THE TIMOTHY INITIATIVE

Homiletics

Henry Oursler
and The Timothy Initiative Staff

Homiletics
Book Two in TTI's Foundational Curriculum

© 2012 by The Timothy Initiative

International Standard Book Number: 978-1477576137

All rights reserved. Published and Printed in the United States of America.

Library of Congress Cataloging-in-Publication Data

No part of this book covered by the copyrights heron may be reproduced or copied
in any form or by any means without written permission of the publisher.

Scripture quotations are from: The New King James Version
Copyright © 1979, 1980, 1982 by Thomas Nelson, Inc.
Used by permission. All rights reserved.

First Edition-North America
Second Edition

Acknowledgements

TTI gives special gratitude to the Docent Group and the leadership of Glenn Lucke and Jared Wilson (Docent Executive Editor for this project). The Docent writer, Wyman Richardson worked hard on this project. TTI is very grateful for Dr. Henry Oursler and his extensive writing and outstanding recreation of this document. Dr. Oursler is a world evangelical leader in this field and his fine work will be used by God to train thousands of church planters.

TTI also gives thanks to Dr. David Nelms, our Founder/President for his vision and influence to see this New Curriculum written. Dr. Nelms has lived humbly to see you succeed greatly in Jesus Christ.

We express our gratitude for the fine, long editorial labor to TTI Executive Editor and Director, Dr. Greg Kappas and the Executive Editorial Assistant and International Director, Rev. Jared Nelms. In addition we thank the entire TTI editorial team of Dr. David Nelms, Rev. Jesse Nelms, Rev. Larry Starkey, Rev. Lou Mancari and Dr. David Nichols. Each of you has given such remarkable grace to us and now to these church planters.

TTI is greatly appreciative of the Grace Fellowship elders, pastors, administrative staff, leaders and GF family. TTI was birthed out of this "church for all nations." Thank you for your generosity in launching this exponential network of church planting movements.

TTI's Board of Directors has given us freedom and focus to excel still more. We are deeply moved by these men and women of God. Our TTI investor base of financial and prayer partners extend around the globe. These individuals, churches, ministries, networks, corporations and organizations are essential and strategic to our collective health and Kingdom impact. Thank you!

We thank the TTI Continental Directors, Regional Directors, National Directors and District/Training Center Leaders for your ministry of love and commitment. You are the ones that forge into new and current frontiers with the Gospel. You truly are our heroes.

Finally, we are forever grateful to you, the church planter. You are planting an orchard, a church planting center through your local church that will touch your region and the world with the Gospel of Jesus Christ. We are honored to serve the Lord Jesus Christ and you. You will make a difference for our great God as you multiply healthy churches for His glory. We love you and believe in you!

TTI Staff Team
July 2010

This workbook is the second of ten workbooks which assist in equipping church planting leaders to start churches that saturate a region and help reach every man, woman and child with the Good News of our Lord. Below, is the list of this initial Curriculum.

TTI Curriculum

Workbook Number/Course:

1. Hermeneutics
2. **Homiletics**
3. Church Planting (New Testament – Acts, Evangelism, Discipleship, Spiritual Life, T4T)
4. Old Testament 1
5. Old Testament 2
6. New Testament Gospels
7. New Testament Pastoral Epistles
8. New Testament General Letters
9. Major Bible Doctrines
10. Apologetics-Church History-Spiritual Warfare

Table of Contents

Introduction 6
Chapter 1: What is Biblical Preaching? 8
Chapter 2: The Communication Process 14
Chapter 3: Learning to Preach Like Jesus 20
Chapter 4: Preparing Our Spirits 24
Chapter 5: Preparing Our Hearts 31
Chapter 6: Preparing Our Minds 37
Chapter 7: Developing an Application-Centered Mindset 43
Chapter 8: Developing Your Homiletical Style 50
Chapter 9: The Big Idea 54
Chapter 10: Sermon Points that Make a Point 58
Chapter 11: Introductions, Conclusions and Illustrations 62
Chapter 12: Outlining and Organizing 66
Chapter 13: The Role of the Holy Spirit in Preaching 70
Chapter 14: Delivery Skills 74
Chapter 15: Growing as a Communicator 78
Chapter 16: Five Warnings to Preachers 82
Chapter 17: Developing and Training Others to Preach 85
Chapter 18: Questions and Answers 87
Appendix 1: Sermon Outlines 89
Appendix 2: Web-based Resources 104
Endnotes 105

Introduction

Congratulations! To be called by God to plant churches is one of the most excellent callings a man can have. Paul talks about the office of leadership (elder, overseer) in *1 Timothy* where he writes, *"If a man desires the office of a bishop, it is a good work" (3:1)*. And one of the most critical components in the description of a church planter and pastor is that of preaching.

Paul later wrote to this pastor and church planter:

> *I charge you therefore before God and the Lord Jesus Christ, who will judge the living and the dead at His appearing and His kingdom: Preach the word! Be ready in season and out of season. Convince, rebuke, exhort, with all longsuffering and teaching. For the time will come when they will not endure sound doctrine, but according to their own desires, because they have itching ears, they will have for themselves teachers; and they will turn their ears away from the truth and be turned aside to fables. But you be watchful in all things, endure afflictions, do the work of an evangelist, fulfill your ministry. For I am already being poured out as a drink offering, and the time of my departure is at hand. I have fought the good fight, I have finished the race, I have kept the faith. Finally, there is laid up for me the crown of righteousness, which the Lord, the righteous Judge, will give to me on that Day, and not to me only but also to all who have loved His appearing. (2 Tim. 4:1-8)*

Please notice seven observations[1] from this passage:

1. Preaching is of utmost importance

Paul began this passage by saying, *"I charge you before God and the Lord Jesus Christ."(4:1)*. Preaching is serious business. It was central to Timothy's calling as a pastor and church planter.

2. We are to preach the Word of God, not our own message

This is how your church will be built to maturity.

3. We are to be ready

We must study, prepare and work hard at preaching. When young men start out preaching, it takes them a while to find their own style and to develop the ability to be a good communicator. Keep working at it. Keep improving. Don't give up. Trust God to make you into a strong preacher.

4. Preaching is built on sound doctrine

Some will fall away from the faith, *"not wanting to endure sound doctrine, but have their ears tickled." (4:3)*. We must remain faithful to God. Our message must always be in accordance with the truth of the Word of God.

5. Preaching requires commitment

We must be sober-minded and endure hardship to fulfill our ministry. There will be hard and discouraging times. Stay focused on the Lord Jesus Christ. Allow Him to encourage you in your preaching.

6. Preaching is the work of an evangelist

Our preaching must be centered in the Gospel, telling others about Jesus, His love and salvation for them.

7. Preaching will be rewarded

Paul talked about the *"crown of righteousness"* (*4:8*), which he anticipated receiving because of His faithful service to Jesus.

> **Assignment:**
>
> Go back and read *2 Tim. 4:1-8* out loud. Read it slowly. Read it as if God is speaking these words directly to you. Which of the seven observations that were listed were most meaningful to you? Why?
>
> Who is the church planter or pastor you know who best models these seven principles? How does he do that?
>
> Now take a few moments and pray the thoughts of *2 Tim. 4:1-8* back to God, asking Him to make you a faithful preacher and communicator of His Word.

Chapter 1
What Is Biblical Preaching?

It was the opening morning of our International Church Planters Summit in India. We had traveled half way around the world to get there. But the one hundred and fifty church planters in attendance had also traveled quite a distance, some for two days, just to be there.

Arjuna Chiguluri, the director of Vision Nationals Ministry, began our session with a great exposition of the Great Commission. It was not only inspiring; it was also deeply Biblical and theological. Arjuna does not speak on a surface level! I came away from that session thinking, "That was a great sermon. That was a classic example of what Biblical preaching is all about."

So what is Biblical preaching? In order to understand a concept clearly, you must first understand its definition. So we begin with a definition of Biblical preaching.

1. The Definition of Biblical Preaching

A. Biblical preaching is the art and science of taking the timeless and inerrant truths of the Word of God.

B. Biblical preaching is through the diligent study and God-shaped personality of the communicator.

C. Biblical preaching is by the work of the Holy Spirit who both: empowers and guides the speaker, and enlightens and convicts the audience.

D. Biblical preaching is to produce genuine faith, true repentance and life-change in the hearts of those hearing the message.

E. Biblical preaching is for the glory of God, the building up of the church, and the spreading of the Gospel to the ends of the earth.[2]

Biblical preaching is both an art and a science. It is a science in the sense that there are rules and principles of communication that we are to follow. It is an art in that each person brings his own unique personality and style to the preaching experience. A renowned British theologian once said, *"Preaching is truth through personality."*[3] Both are necessary.

Also, Biblical preaching is centered around and takes its content from the inerrant Word of God

It is God's truth that we proclaim. *1 The. 2:13* says, *"For this reason we also thank God without ceasing, because when you received the word of God which you heard from us, you welcomed it not as the word of men, but as it is in truth, the word of God, which also effectively works in you."*

His Word is timeless. *Psa. 119:89* says, *"Forever, O Lord, Your Word is settled in heaven."*

His Word is inerrant. Jesus said, *"Your word is truth."* (*Joh. 17:17*)

> NOTES

A. <u>Biblical preaching begins with a diligent study of the Scriptures</u>
   Paul told Timothy, *"Be diligent to present yourself approved to God, a worker who does not need to be ashamed, rightly dividing the word of truth."* (*2 Tim. 2:15*) Those who have the gift of teaching the Bible must also possess the gift and/or commitment of studying the Bible. Solomon, the writer of the Old Testament book of Ecclesiastes said, *"In addition to being a wise man, the Preacher also taught the people knowledge; and he pondered, searched out and arranged many proverbs. The Preacher sought to find delightful words and to write words of truth correctly."* (*12:9-10*) It took time to compose a message that would make an impact in people's lives.

   Biblical preaching also comes through the personality of the preacher. Some communicators are encouragers, some are confrontational. Some use humor, while others use sound logic and well-reasoned content. Do not fall into the trap of trying to mimic your favorite preacher. Learn from them, but develop your own style as a communicator.

B. <u>Biblical preaching is empowered by the work of the Holy Spirit</u>
   He empowers and guides the speaker.
   - The Holy Spirit is our comforter, helper and aid. (*Joh. 14:16-17*)
   - The Holy Spirit fills and empowers us. (*Eph. 5:18*)
   - The Holy Spirit teaches us God's Word. (*Joh. 14:26*)

   He also enlightens and convicts those who are listening:
   - The Holy Spirit brings life and breath. (see *Eze. 37*)
   - The Holy Spirit convicts the world of sin, righteousness and judgment. (*Joh. 16:8-11; Isa. 6:1-7*)
   - The Holy Spirit glorifies God and enlightens His truth to all. (*Joh. 16:14-15*)

C. <u>Biblical preaching produces fruit</u>
   There will be genuine faith, true repentance and life-change in the hearts of those hearing the message.
   - When Nathan the prophet delivered God's message to King David, he repented and sought God's forgiveness. (*Psa. 32, 51*)
   - When he heard God's message, Isaiah repented and declared himself ruined and undone. (*Isa. 6:5*)
   - When the Samaritan woman heard Jesus' words by the well of water near Sychar, she repented, believed and told the whole city about Jesus. (*Joh. 4*)

NOTES

- When the Thessalonians heard the Gospel, they responded as follows:

For our gospel did not come to you in word only, but also in power and in the Holy Spirit and with full conviction; just as you know what kind of men we proved to be among you for your sake. You also became imitators of us and of the Lord, having received the word in much tribulation with the joy of the Holy Spirit, so that you became an example to all the believers in Macedonia and in Achaia. For the word of the Lord has sounded forth from you, not only in Macedonia and Achaia, but also in every place your faith toward God has gone forth, so that we have no need to say anything. For they themselves report about us what kind of a reception we had with you, and how you turned to God from idols to serve a living and true God, and to wait for His Son from heaven. (1 The. 1:5-10)

True Biblical preaching aims at life change. Unbelievers will come to faith in Jesus, and Christians will respond with true repentance in hearing the message.

    D. <u>Biblical preaching ultimately has three goals</u>:
To glorify God, to build up the church, and to spread the Gospel to the ends of the earth.

Our ultimate purpose in life is to glorify God. (*1 Cor. 10:31*) *Isa. 46:10* tells us that when God's Word is preached, His purposes will be accomplished. And *Isa. 55:11* says, *"So shall My word be that goes forth from My mouth: it shall not return to Me void, but it shall accomplish what I please, and it shall prosper in the thing for which I sent it."*

As you plant your church, you will notice that preaching the Gospel builds the church to maturity and reaches lost people with the message of salvation. The church is built on *the apostle's teaching*. (*Act. 2:42-47*)

2. What Biblical Preaching Is Not

Sometimes it is helpful to understand a concept by looking at what it is not.

    A. <u>Biblical preaching is not entertainment</u>
Though people gladly heard Jesus teach, His purpose was not to entertain them. His purpose was to declare the Gospel and preach the Kingdom of God.

    B. <u>Biblical preaching is not self-help therapy</u>
It is not worldly advice designed to help people live better lives.

    C. <u>Biblical preaching is not "feel-good theology"</u>
There are so-called Bible teachers today who proclaim a health-and-wealth gospel, sometimes known as Prosperity Theology. Their message is that God wants you to be completely healthy and rich. In direct contradiction to the Word of God, their message appeals simply to men's fleshly desires. False gospels tell us what we want to hear. The true Gospel tells us what we need to hear.

D. Biblical preaching is not "information-only"
Our preaching in our new church must contain content, but it must be more than that. We are not called to inform people with facts, but to preach to their hearts, expecting a response of faith. Biblical preaching must always be directed toward application. We don't just proclaim truth, we proclaim truth to people. We don't just teach the Bible, we teach the Bible to people. We don't just preach content, we preach for life-change in our new churches and those that we multiply. We will discuss this more in-depth later in this manual.

E. Biblical preaching is not to be taken lightly
We are called to devote ourselves to study and preparation, accurately handling the Word of God. There are some today who refuse to prepare at all, trusting that God's Spirit will direct them in what to say when they get up to speak. However, as we have already seen, we are called to study hard, to craft our words carefully and to trust God's Spirit to direct us in our study, planning and preparation as well as when we deliver our message.

3. The Biblical Basis for Preaching

Biblical preaching is Christ-centered preaching. It is preaching that lifts up Jesus and what He has done for us.

A. Christ-centered preaching is centered on the cross (*1 Cor. 1:18-25*)
All true preaching must ultimately come back to the cross and what Jesus has done for our sin-problem. This is the message that we are called to preach. This is the reason that we must establish new churches; to faithfully and effectively proclaim the greatest news ever announced. We must always bring our audiences back to the Gospel message.

Tim Dunham, who serves Jesus by leading a church planting movement in Thailand, recently presented a sermon entitled "*Identity Crisis*," where He talked about Jesus' identity as the Son of God, and then the offer He makes to us to come to Him in simple faith and obedience for salvation.

As you prepare your sermon messages, ask yourself, "In what ways does the Gospel relate to what I am talking about? How can I share a clear, compelling presentation of the Gospel to this sermon?"

B. Christ-centered preaching humbles man and exalts Jesus (*1 Cor. 1:26-31*)
Jesus said when He is lifted up, He will draw all men to Himself. (*Joh. 12:32*) Man's sin is centered on his pride and self-sufficiency. Biblical preaching destroys our pride and exalts our Savior.

C. The preacher must be culturally sensitive in his style (*1 Cor. 2:1-5*)
You must know your culture, understand your audience, and relate the timeless truths of the Word of God to people in a way that they understand.

This is one of the reasons why you must raise up future church planters from within your church. They are the ones who know their culture best.

> **NOTES**

They are the ones who have contacts and relationships with people in their villages and towns.

In my thirty-five years of ministry, I've found that the people who relate best to non-Christians are those who are recent converts. Help them learn how to articulate the Gospel to those who need to hear.

D. <u>Christ-centered preachers speak as fathers</u> (*1 Cor. 4:14-15*) Fathers care for their children. Christ-centered church planting preachers care for the people in their church and community. They seek to love them, lead them to Christ, and help them grow to maturity in their faith and effectiveness in their service to Christ.

E. <u>Fatherly Christ-centered preaching aims for transformed lives</u> (*Col. 1:24-29*) Your preaching will help build the body of Christ to maturity (see *Eph.4:11-16*).

Some of the people to whom you preach may become leaders and church planters for your church multiplication ministry. As you preach, you are teaching others who will ultimately teach others who will multiply the message to others.

That's the way God designed the church to grow. In *2 Tim. 2:2*, Paul instructed Timothy to take the things he had learned from Paul and teach them to faithful men who would be able to teach others also. Your message must be designed to help leaders grow to maturity and to reproduce themselves in the lives of others, who will reproduce their lives in others also.

Chuwang Davou, who directs the Centre for Leadership Development headquartered in Nigeria, has given a lot of thought to the process of development as men and women submit themselves for training in church planting. He teaches that we must have a specific strategy to bring potential leaders through to maturity and focuses on three elements:
- Leadership Character: A heart in tune with God's Spirit.
- Leadership Values: A head that understands God's plan.
- Leadership Skills: Hands that do God's will.

Assignment:

This chapter listed numerous Bible references. Take your Bible and look up each reference, making note of what it says about God, truth, preaching and mankind.

God:

Truth:

Preaching:

Mankind:

List your reasons for preaching a Bible-centered message. What are the benefits of this approach?

What was the biggest lesson you learned about Biblical preaching in this chapter?

How did Paul and the other early church leaders preach the Bible? What can we learn from them as we plant new churches? Discuss.

NOTES

Chapter 2
The Communication Process

1. Introduction

Nigeria is home to one of my favorite people in the world. He is a church planter in Jalingo, Nigeria. The first time I met him, our team had just traveled seven hours through dangerous country on roads with potholes big enough to swallow the car we were in. I am glad to say we survived "the road to Jalingo."

When we arrived in Jalingo, the first thing we did was to visit my friend at his church service. To say they had a celebration going on would be an understatement! There was spirited singing, heart-felt praying, and dancing. Oh, was there dancing! The pastor and his congregation danced for joy before the Lord. And then he got up to preach. I sat there captivated, listening to this servant of Jesus proclaim the Gospel. He was energetic, clear, and engaging.

"It is a sin to bore people with the Bible!"[4] We possess the greatest news ever announced. In fact, that's what the word "*gospel*" means, *Good News!*

- A. <u>God has chosen us to proclaim His Word to others</u>
  - *"So then faith comes by hearing, and hearing by the word of God."* (Rom. 10:17)
  - *"You did not choose me, but I chose you and appointed you that you should go and bear fruit, and that your fruit should remain, that whatever you ask the Father in My name He may give it to you."* (Joh. 15:16)

- B. <u>God uses us to communicate His message</u>
  He has given us His inerrant and infallible Word, spiritual gifts, talents and desires, a passion to communicate for His glory, and open doors for effective ministry.

  When we use the terms inerrant and infallible to describe the Word of God, it means that the Word of God is perfect. It is without error and completely true. That assurance gives confidence that the message we preach is from God and not invented by man.

  I was able to interview a respected pastor several years ago. I asked him what he felt made him an effective communicator. His response was great:

  > *I have this burning passion never to be out of touch with my times. I want my communication to be so clear that the public is stunned to realize how eternally relevant God and His Word really are.*[5]

C. <u>We must work hard to become the best communicators of the Gospel that we can be for God's glory</u>
In a survey[6] done at the University of California at Los Angeles, researchers sought to determine why people respond to certain speakers. They found that only 7% is the result of the words we say, and fully 93% is how the message is communicated. That tells me that we must give special attention not only to what is said, but how it is being said. Our attitudes, manner, behavior, sincerity and delivery are very important.

2. Why Communication?

A. <u>Talk so people will listen</u>
God has ordained that the way the Gospel is spread around the world and the way His Word is taught in new and existing churches is through public proclamation.

"For whoever calls on the name of the Lord shall be saved. How then shall they call on Him in whom they have not believed? And how shall they believe in Him of whom they have not heard? And how shall they hear without a preacher? And how shall they preach unless they are sent? As it is written: How beautiful are the feet of those who preach the gospel of peace, who bring glad tidings of good things!" (Rom. 10:13-15)

B. <u>To make our message clear</u>
It is very important that our audience hears the Gospel clearly, accurately and relevantly. This becomes the prayer of the Apostle Paul:
- *"Continue earnestly in prayer, being vigilant in it with thanksgiving; meanwhile praying also for us, that God would open to us a door for the word, **to speak** the mystery of Christ, for which I am also in chains, that I may make it manifest, as I ought to speak. Walk in wisdom toward those who are outside, redeeming the time. Let **your speech** always be with grace, seasoned with salt, that you may know how you ought to answer each one." (Col. 4:2-6)*
  ▶ There are actually two forms of communication in this passage, marked in bold letters. The phrase *to speak* refers to public speaking, as in standing in front of an audience and preaching to them. The second phrase, *your speech*, refers to daily conversation, speaking to one individual at a time. In both cases, Paul asks for prayer that he would *know how I ought to speak and how to answer each one*.

C. <u>To relate the Bible as it is to people as they are</u>
Paul spoke on Mars Hill to the Athenian philosophers. His message was geared to their interests and backgrounds. By God's grace, there was a positive response:
- *"And when they heard of the resurrection of the dead, some mocked, while others said, 'We will hear you again on this matter.' So Paul departed from among them. However, some men joined him and believed, among them Dionysius the Areopagite, a woman named Damaris, and others with them." (Act. 17:32-34)*

> **NOTES**

Some mocked, some believed, and others wanted to hear more. Interestingly, one of those who believed was Dionysius, who later became the church leader for the entire city of Athens. It started with Paul finding the common things between them, and then faithfully proclaiming the Gospel.

    D. <u>To give people more than information</u>
Paul poured his life into those he taught:
- *"We loved you so much that we were delighted to share with you not only the gospel of God but our lives as well, because you had become so dear to us."* (*1 The. 2:8*)

3. The Seven Stages of the Communication Process

Most textbooks about public speaking will describe seven stages in the communication process. This is very helpful to understand when we are speaking in public.

    A. <u>Speaker Internalization</u>
It begins with the speaker applying the message into his life. The Greek philosopher Aristotle taught that there are three elements in communication.[7] He used the Greek words *logos, pathos,* and *ethos* to describe them. To these I would add a fourth element: theos. Let me define each of these for you and show you how relevant they are as we teach the Bible.
- <u>Logos</u>: this is the "content" element. The Greek word *logos*, means *word* or *content*. You must have something to say! When it comes to Biblical communication, this is critical, because the content comes from God's Word.

Your favorite Bible teacher may be strongest in *logos*. He knows the Word well. He communicates it so that others learn what it says and are transformed by its teachings.

Arjuna Chiguluri, the director of Vision Nationals Ministry, is exceptionally strong in *logos*. Having studied at Talbot Theological Seminary, he is well versed in the truths of the Bible. One of the ministries of Vision Nationals is The Master's Seminary, where Arjuna and his team of Bible teachers train young men for the ministry.
- <u>Pathos</u>: this is the "emotional" element of communication. The Greek word *pathos* means *feelings, emotions and desires*. It involves feeling deeply, not only about the truth, but especially about the people to whom you are preaching. A person strong in *pathos* communicates his care and concern for the sheep under his care. He is known for his compassion for people.

Kibera is one of the largest slums in the world. Located just outside the city of Nairobi, Kenya, it measures one kilometer by one kilometer in dimension, with over 1.5 million people living there. Several years ago four of us were visiting there, meeting with a group of 25 pastors. As we talked, it became apparent to me how much these men cared for the people of their city. They poured out their hearts about the need for teaching, training and leadership development in the areas of church planting and church

growth. They cared, and God is blessing their ministry.
- Ethos: this is the element that emphasizes the preacher's "character." The Greek word *ethos* speaks of someone having *character, honesty and integrity*. He is a man of spotless character, acting consistently with what he teaches.

Have you ever met a man of faultless character? His impact is immediate, because he reflects the holiness and righteousness of Jesus. I met such a man several years ago. He was from a country where there is extreme persecution of Christians, and he has suffered for Jesus. Yet, he has not compromised his commitment to his Lord. He provides leadership for an underground church movement that reaches many people today.

- Theos: because we are talking about communication that is distinctively Christian, this element emphasizes the genuine touch of God in the preacher's life. The Greek word *theos* is the word for God. Here I am using it in the sense that God has truly touched and made a difference in someone's life. He has *charisma*, the sense that the Holy Spirit is truly empowering and directing His life and ministry. *Charisma* means a spiritual power or personal quality that gives an individual influence or authority as he ministers the Word of God to others.

Dr. Joon Jon Kim of Seoul, Korea, is a man of God. I remember meeting him and his wife at his office years ago. I was struck with the fact that he was deeply a man of prayer. Prayer saturated everything that he and his team did. He understood that the Holy Spirit must empower him and work through his life if there was to be lasting ministry.

These four elements ought to be present in the life of every pastor and church planter. However, you most likely are strongest in one of them. Throughout your ministry, as you internalize the truths you are preaching, you will grow in each of these four areas.

B. Words
Once we internalize the truth of the passage we are teaching, we begin to put those concepts into language that will communicate to our audience. The use of words is very important: keep your sermon simple, using words that your audience will understand.

As you read through the Gospels, notice how Jesus communicated. He used words and images that His audience could relate to: *a farmer going out to sow seeds in the field, a lost coin, a wedding, a widow asking a judge for justice*. In doing so, He was able to communicate deep biblical truth to an audience that could relate and understand it.

C. Speech
Now you begin to preach your sermon. Here are some quick suggestions:
- Speak clearly so people will understand you.
- Speak loud enough so people will be able to hear you.
- Be enthusiastic. You are preaching the greatest news ever!

NOTES

- Be clear in the organization of your sermon so people will be able to follow you.
- Be yourself. Allow your personality to come through in your teaching.

D. <u>Distractions</u>

As you speak there will inevitably be distractions. There are three types of distractions:

Some distractions will come from the surrounding environment, such as a baby crying in the audience. Do your best to keep people's attention despite these issues.

Other distractions will come from people's individual lives. Perhaps they are sick or have a cold. Others might be tired or preoccupied with other things. A lively and enthusiastic presentation will help them focus on what you are saying.

But finally there is a third type of distraction that is spiritual in nature. Satan attempts to confuse people's minds. He wants them to think about anything other than the truths you are talking about. This is where we must pray and ask God to stop Satan's activities, and to give an open door to people's lives so they will respond.

E. <u>Listening</u>

Some people love to listen to people talk. Others don't. But there are things we can do – and things we can avoid – to help increase the effectiveness of our communication:
- Problems can occur when we have too many points in our messages. Remember, keep it simple.
- Problems can occur when we speak too long. This varies from culture to culture. Just remember to honor your listeners and not speak so long that they fall asleep.
- Speak clearly and loudly. Change the rate of your speech, from fast to slow. Change the volume of your speaking voice, from loud to soft.
- Use illustrations that will keep their attention.

F. <u>Listener internalization</u>

Here your listeners attempt to internalize the message into their lives. You will aid them in this process by using good illustrations and making points of application to their personal lives. Many times preachers tell their flocks *what* to do, but they fail to show them *how* to do it. We'll devote an entire chapter later in this book to the whole idea of application.

G. <u>Feedback</u>
Finally, the communication process is complete when you as a speaker receive feedback to your message. Feedback can occur in a variety of forms: *questions they ask, commitments they make, changed behavior, people trusting Christ as their Savior, etc.* Feedback might even be as simple as smiles on their faces.

It is critical for you to receive proper feedback. Ask people to give you feedback to your sermons. Ask them questions like:
- *"What did you understand in my sermon?"*
- *"What was clear?" "What wasn't clear?"*
- *"How can I do better next time?"*

Assignment:

This chapter discussed four elements to good communication: *logos, pathos, ethos* and *theos*.

Which of those is your strongest area?

In what ways is that strength demonstrated in your life and ministry?

What is your weakest area?

What are you doing to strengthen that area of your life and ministry?

Now discuss these answers with a friend who knows you well. Do they agree with your personal assessment? Why or why not?

Chapter 3
Learning to Preach Like Jesus [8]

1. Introduction

Jesus' preaching attracted enormous crowds, and the Bible often records the positive reactions of those crowds to His teaching.

At the conclusion of the Sermon on the Mount (*Mat. 5-7*), *7:28-29* tells us: *"the people were astonished at His teaching, for He taught them as one having authority, and not as the scribes."* *Mat. 22:33* records the same response: *"And when the multitudes heard this, they were astonished at His teaching"*. This word means they were very impressed, caught off guard, surprised and delighted. *Mat. 12:37* says, *"the common people heard Him gladly."*

People enjoyed listening to Jesus preach and teach. They had never heard anyone speak to them the way Jesus did. They were captivated by His speaking.

To capture the attention of men and women like Jesus did, we must communicate spiritual truth the way He did. Jesus must be our model for preaching. In *Joh. 12:49* Jesus admitted, *"I have not spoken on My own authority, but the Father who sent Me gave Me a command, what I should say and what I should speak."*

There is so much to learn from Jesus' style of communication. In this chapter we will discover three attributes of Jesus' preaching.

2. Jesus Began with People's Needs, Hurts and Interests

Jesus often taught in response to a question or a pressing problem from someone in the crowd. He addressed the points of interest and need that His audience had. His preaching had immediacy about it. He was always relevant and always on target for that moment.

When Jesus preached His first sermon at Nazareth, He read from the prophet Isaiah to announce what the preaching agenda of His ministry would be:

> *So He came to Nazareth, where He had been brought up. And as His custom was, He went into the synagogue on the Sabbath day, and stood up to read. And He was handed the book of the prophet Isaiah. And when He had opened the book, He found the place where it was written: 'The Spirit of the Lord is upon Me, because He has anointed Me to preach the gospel to the poor; He has sent Me to heal the brokenhearted to proclaim liberty to the captives and recovery of sight to the blind, to set at liberty those who are oppressed; to proclaim the acceptable year of the Lord' (Luk. 4:16-19).*

Please read those words carefully and notice that Jesus' emphasis was on meeting needs and healing hurts. He had Good News to share, and people responded to it because He began where they were, in their needs, hurts and interests. Our message to the lost must be good news. If it isn't good news, it isn't the Gospel!

A. By beginning with people's needs when you preach, you immediately gain the attention of your audience. Practically every communicator understands and uses this principle. Wise teachers know to start with the students' interests and move them toward the lesson. Effective salesmen know you always start with the customer, not the product. Smart managers know to begin with the employee's complaint, not their own agenda. You start where people are and move them to where you want them to be.

B. Your audience determines how you start your message. When Paul spoke to the group of secular philosopher's on Mars Hill in Acts 17, He did not begin with biblical presuppositions. He started where they were, asking the questions they were asking. He used specific words they would understand. He even quoted several of their secular philosophers. He ultimately directed His message toward the resurrection of Jesus, the message they needed to hear.

C. It is important to realize, however, that even though Jesus started with people's needs, hurts and interests, He didn't stay there. He pointed them to God. He taught them the truth.

3. Jesus Related Truth to Life

I love the practicality and simplicity of Jesus' teaching. It was clear, relevant and applicable. He aimed for application because His goal was to transform people, not merely inform them.

The deepest kind of teaching is that which makes a difference in people's day-to-day lives. As Dwight L. Moody once said, *The Bible was not given to increase our knowledge but to change our lives.*[9] The goal is Christ-like character.

I love to teach theology without telling people it is theology and without using theological terms. I've preached sermon series on the incarnation, justification, sanctification and Christology without ever using the terms!

How does that work? It works because truth is incredibly practical. Truth has a way of addressing the deepest needs of our lives. But too many preachers fail to make the connection between theology and life. We need our preachers to be good translators, taking the timeless truths of the Word of God and translating them in a way that makes sense in our day-to-day lives.

4. Jesus Spoke to the Crowd with an Interesting Style

The crowds loved to listen to Jesus. *Mat.12:37* says: *"The common people heard Him gladly"*. The term "common people," refers to the normal, uneducated and untrained people of the day. They listened with delight when Jesus spoke.

In a previous chapter, I made the point that the goal of Biblical preaching is not "entertainment." And that's true. The goal is transformation by the Word of God through the work of the Spirit of God. However, if you look up the word *entertain* in a dictionary, you will find this definition: *capturing and holding the attention for an extended period of time*. I don't know any preacher who doesn't want to do that! We shouldn't be afraid of being interesting. A sermon doesn't have to be dry to be spiritual.

To the unchurched, dull preaching is unforgivable. Truth poorly delivered is ignored. It never ceases to amaze me how some Bible teachers are able to take the most exciting book in the world and bore people to tears with it. As I've said previously, it is a sin to bore people with the Bible.

The problem is this: when I teach God's Word in an uninteresting way, people don't just think *I'm* boring. They think *God* is boring! We slander God's character if we preach with an uninspiring style or tone. The message is too important to share it with an uninterested attitude. This weight of preaching and teaching the Word of God must be faced. We do not make the Word of God relevant; we discover its relevance and communicate the Scriptures in a relevant way to our culture(s).

Jesus captured the interest of large crowds with techniques that you and I can use:

A. First, He told stories to make a point. Jesus was a master story-teller. He'd state a point, and then tell a parable to teach that truth. In fact, the Bible shows that story-telling was Jesus' favorite technique when speaking to a crowd. *"All these things Jesus spoke to the multitude in parables; and without a parable He did not speak to them."* (Mat. 13:34) Somehow preachers have forgotten that the Bible is essentially a book of stories! That's how God has chosen to communicate His Word to human beings.

There are many benefits to using stories to communicate spiritual truth. Stories hold our attention. They stir our emotions. They impact us in ways that precepts and propositions never do. If you want to change lives, you must craft the message for impact, not for information. Stories help us remember. Long after the outline of our sermon is forgotten, people will remember the stories behind the sermon.

It's fascinating to watch how quickly a crowd tunes in whenever a speaker begins telling a story and how quickly that attention vanishes as soon as the story is finished!

B. Second, Jesus used simple language. He didn't use technical or theological jargon. He spoke in simple terms that normal people could understand. He used the street language of His day and talked about birds, flowers, lost coins, and other everyday objects that anyone could relate to.

Jesus taught profound truths in simple ways. Today we do the opposite. We teach simple truths in profound ways, and the result is confusion, disinterest and rejection.

I believe simple sermon outlines are always the strongest outlines. I consider being called a simple preacher to be a compliment. I'm interested in seeing lives changed, not in impressing people with technical language and confusing concepts. I'd rather be clear than complex.

Jesus, not anyone else, must be our model for effective communication. When we preach and teach like Jesus did, we will see the results He did.

Assignment:

Jesus' most famous sermon is known as The Sermon on the Mount. It is recorded both in Matthew and Luke. Matthew's version is recorded in *chapters 5-7*. Take your Bible and read this sermon out loud. As you do, take a few notes. Write down what you see in these verses about the way Jesus spoke, the images that He used, and the way people responded to Him.

NOTES

Chapter 4
Preparing Our Spirits: Are You Called to Preach?

1. Introduction

I was speaking at one of our International Church Planter Summits[10] in Jos, Nigeria. God had blessed the ministry there and we had over 250 church planters and church planting movement leaders from all over the country and several from surrounding countries.

I had the privilege of meeting with many of these great men of God and hearing the stories about how God had called them into the ministry and how he was using them, even in the midst of severe persecution.

There were five men I especially remember, because they were serving Jesus in a difficult area where their lives were constantly in danger. I asked one of them, *"Why are you doing this?"* He responded:

> *Jesus has saved me from my life of sin. My life will never be the same. I feel compelled to tell my fellow countrymen who are caught up in the different religious traditions that they must believe in Jesus. He is the only way!*

What a great testimony. He and his fellow church planters were serving Jesus in a very hostile area. And what kept them going each day, even in the face of severe persecution, was their call to ministry.

I've found that knowing and being able to clearly articulate your call is an important factor for all church planters. Let's take a moment and go back to the New Testament to see the example of another young church planter.

Timothy was a young disciple. Some commentators believe he was still a teenager. But Paul saw something in his life that gave him the confidence that Timothy would become a great leader, church planter and pastor. He saw God's call on his life.

Because of that, Paul issued some very strong commands to young Timothy. As you read through these commands, take them to heart yourself. These are God's words *to you* as well.

"Let no one despise your youth, but be an example to the believers in word, in conduct, in love, in spirit, in faith, in purity" (*1 Tim. 4:12*). Just because Timothy was young did not mean he was not qualified, gifted and called by God.

"Do not neglect the gift that is in you, which was given to you by prophecy with the laying on of the hands of the eldership" (*1 Tim. 4:14*). The elders had recognized and affirmed the calling that Timothy had received, and they publicly acknowledged him as a called servant of Jesus Christ. However, Paul knew that when Timothy was under

pressure and hard times came in the ministry (as they always will), he would need to remember his calling and the ministry God had given him.

"Guard, through the Holy Spirit who dwells in us, the treasure which has been entrusted to you" (2 Tim. 1:14).

"Be diligent to present yourself approved to God, a worker who does not need to be ashamed, rightly dividing the word of truth" (2 Tim. 2:15). This verse tells us that even though Timothy was gifted, he would still have to work hard to fulfill his ministry. Church planting is challenging. Preaching is difficult. There are times you may not *feel* like working hard in the ministry. Remember the One who has called you. Remember the task to which He has called you. Remember those whom you serve in your church.

Let's take a few minutes to examine what is involved in God's calling in our lives.

2. What Does It Mean To Be Called By God?

Do you remember the story of God calling another young boy named Samuel? Take the time right now to go back and read *1 Samuel 3:1-21*. This passage tells how the Lord called Samuel to be a prophet, the prophet who would anoint the first two legitimate kings of Israel. The passage begins with the statement that *"the word of the Lord was rare in those days."* But that was about to change.

The Lord calls Samuel three times, each call increasing in intensity. But Samuel thinks it is only his foster father Eli who is calling. Finally the elderly Eli perceives that it is actually God calling the young boy, and Samuel receives his first communication from the Lord.

Assignment:

Read *1 Samuel 3:1-21*.

How did God call Samuel?

How did God call you?

How did Samuel learn to hear the voice of God?

How are you learning to hear the voice of God?

NOTES

NOTES

John Newton, the 18th-century Anglican clergyman and writer of the famous hymn "Amazing Grace," noted three indications of a call.[11] First, a call to ministry is accompanied by *"a warm and earnest desire to be employed in this service."* Second, a call to ministry is accompanied by *"some competent sufficiency as to gifts, knowledge, and utterance."* And third, a call to ministry is accompanied by *"a correspondent opening in Providence, by a gradual train of circumstances pointing out the means, the time, the place, of actually entering upon the work."*

George Whitefield, the 18th-century evangelist, gives this advice for those considering a call:

> *Ask yourselves again and again whether you would preach for Christ if you were sure to lay down your life for so doing? If you fear the displeasure of a man for doing your duty now, assure yourselves you are not yet thus minded.*[12]

To be called by God means we are called into a relationship with Him and called to minister *for Him*. This was true in the life of young Samuel. He grew in his relationship with the Lord and the Lord's presence was with him; and he also saw God use him in a mighty way in serving God throughout Israel.

Mark 3:14 tells us about Jesus calling the twelve disciples to follow Him. *"Then He appointed twelve, that they might be with Him and that He might send them out to preach."* Notice the two aspects of this calling: they were called to be in relationship *with* Jesus and they were called to minister *for* Jesus.

John 15:16 records another similar statement by Jesus: *"You did not choose Me, but I chose you and appointed you that you should go and bear fruit, and that your fruit should remain, that whatever you ask the Father in My name He may give you."*

This statement was made right after Jesus described the priority of their relationship *with Him, by abiding in Him*. To *abide* means to remain in a fixed and permanent relationship with Jesus. Just like the vine must remain permanently attached to the branch and draw its life-sustenance from the branch, we must remain in a life-giving relationship with Jesus every day of our lives.

They were to bear fruit in their ministry. The context tells us this fruit would be the changed lives of people they reached in their ministry, and so it is with us as church planters. We want to see changed lives by reaching new people with the Gospel.

3. What Are the Distinguishing Marks of God's Call?

It is important to realize that God deals with each of us uniquely and individually. No two calls are exactly the same. However, there are five common principles that we can notice.

> A. <u>A sincere love for Jesus and evidence of growth in Him</u>
> Do you remember the story of Peter in *John 21*? He had denied Jesus three times on the night of His crucifixion. Instead of harshly rebuking him, Jesus restores Peter to Himself by asking the same question three times. Do you remember what it is? Jesus asked, *"Do you love Me?"* That was the heart of the issue.

Those who would serve Jesus must demonstrate a supreme love for Him. We don't serve out of obligation, fear or duty. We serve Him because we love Him for who He is and for what He has done for us.

Do you love Jesus? How much? Are you growing in your relationship with Him every day?

B. <u>A continuing passion to serve Jesus</u>
I love to serve Jesus. Usually, it is not hard or painful to minister in His name. For some of you it is very hard and painful, but you gladly accept it with passion and fervor. I am addicted to seeing life-change in people. There is nothing that motivates me more than that. One of the greatest compliments that you can pay me as a preacher is to come up to me six months after I've spoken and tell me how God has used that sermon in your life over the last six months. That's motivating!

My calling to ministry is continually reaffirmed every time I preach and teach. It's just an example of how God has made me.

What about you? Do you have a continuing passion to serve Him? Do you love being used by Him in the lives of other people? Do you do it for His glory, or is your motivation to be in the spotlight and take the fame and applause for yourself?

C. <u>A giftedness to minister effectively</u>
Take a moment right now and read *Ephesians 4:11-16*. The big idea in that passage is that God has given gifted leaders to the church to train others in effective ministry and to equip them for works of service. You are called to be a church planter. Now, are you gifted to be a church planter? Let's look at the text and see what it says about this dynamic aspect of church ministry.

Do you know what your spiritual gifts are? Are you developing those gifts and abilities to their fullest potential? Your participation in this class, and reading this manual are signs that you desire to grow in your effectiveness in ministry. What are other ways you are growing in your ministry expertise?

D. <u>An ability to see the need</u>
In *Isaiah 6*, the prophet is undone by the reality of his sin. He cries out to God for forgiveness and cleansing, which he receives by grace through faith. And then God issues a challenge. The message of the Gospel needs to be proclaimed throughout Israel. *"Who will go for Us? Whom can we send?"* God asks. And Isaiah responds immediately, *"Here am I. Send me!"*

Isaiah immediately saw the need. Others around him saw the problem. But Isaiah, having just received a fresh touch from God, saw how God could use him as His instrument to bring healing, grace and forgiveness to the nation.

Do you see the need in your village and throughout your country? Do you see how God could use you to be an instrument of His grace?

> **NOTES**

E. <u>God's calling is always affirmed by others</u>
We need each other in the body of Christ. *1 Corinthians 12:14-27* tells that God has designed the parts of the body to need each other. One way that happens in leadership development is that the mature and established leaders recognize the gifts and callings in the lives of younger, developing leaders.

Paul mentioned this when he wrote to Timothy: *"Do not neglect the gift that is in you, which was given to you by prophecy with the laying on of the hands of the eldership."* (*1 Tim. 4:14*) The elders had recognized and affirmed the calling that Timothy had received, and they publicly acknowledged him as a called servant of Jesus Christ.

This is both an encouragement and a safeguard. If wise and godly leaders do not see God's hand on your life and ministry, it is prudent not to proceed in church planting. However, if they have encouraged you and blessed you, take that as a sign from God that He is guiding you into the path of His service.

Have you received affirmation and acknowledgement of your gifts and calling by the leaders in your local church? What have they said about you that gives you confidence in following God's call to be a church planter? What are you hearing from those who give an account for your life to God?

4. How Do You Learn to Hear the Voice of God?

Young Samuel had a problem. He did not know how to hear God's voice. In fact, in *1 Samuel 3*, God's voice sounded a lot like a human voice to Samuel. What was he to do? How would he learn to hear the voice of God in his life? I would like to go back to *1 Samuel 3* and see three principles about how we can learn to hear the voice of God in our lives.

A. <u>Principle # 1 – We Must Get Ready to Listen</u>
Hearing God's voice begins with openness. *1 Sam. 3:1* tells us that words from God were rare in those days and that visions were infrequent. I do not believe it was reluctance on God's part to communicate with and bless His people. I believe people's hearts had grown cold and they were not listening for His voice.

But Samuel was attentive. In *3:4-5*, he heard the voice of God and responded, even though he mistakenly thought it was Eli who was calling him.

Chapter 3, verses 7-9 tells us that Samuel did not yet know the Lord, nor had the word of the Lord yet been revealed to him. Obviously Samuel knew *about* God, but He did not yet have a personal relationship with Him.

We get ready to listen to God by confessing our sin and cleansing our hearts

Isa. 59:1-2 tells us, *"Behold, the Lord's hand is not so short that it cannot save; nor is His ear so dull that it cannot hear. But your iniquities have*

made a separation between you and your God, and your sins have hidden His face from you so that He does not hear."

Have you confessed your sin? Have you received His cleansing and forgiveness so there is no separation between you and Him? Is your heart ready to respond when God speaks?

B. <u>Principle # 2 – Grow in Your Faith by Getting into the Word of God</u>
In *1 Sam. 3:10*, Samuel responds to God by saying, *"Speak, for Your servant hears."* God is speaking. The question is: Are you listening? Obviously Samuel listened, and the result, recorded in *verse 19*, is that *"Samuel grew, and the Lord was with him and let none of his words fall to the ground."* There was no irrelevance in Samuel's message to the people. It was right on target. Why? Because he kept growing in His faith and letting God speak to him.

God primarily and supremely speaks to us through His Word. I believe 90% of what you will ever need to hear from God has already been said in the Bible. Whenever you sense God speaking to you, remember this: His words to you will never contradict His Word in the Bible. His subjective message to you will always be confirmed by His objective message in Scripture.

When I was a young Christian, I had a mentor who loved God's Word. He based his entire life on it. Whenever I would talk about doing something or making a decision, he would always ask, *"Do you have a verse for that?"* He wanted me to know for sure that God was speaking to me, and that I could back it up with principles from the Bible.

There are six primary ways we are to interact with God's Word:
- Hear the Word – *2 Tim. 4:2*.
- Read the Word – *2 Tim. 3:16-17*.
- Study the Word – *2 Tim. 2:15*.
- Memorize the Word – *Psa. 119:11; Jos. 1:8*.
- Apply the Word – *Ezr. 7:10*.
- Meditate on and Pray the Word – *Psa. 119*.

C. <u>Principle # 3 – Obey Immediately</u>
There was no hesitation in Samuel's life. When God spoke, he responded. He obeyed immediately.

In *1 Sam. 3:8-10*, we see that he learned to discern that the Lord was speaking and He responded by listening intently. In *verses 15-18*, he told Eli all that had happened and began his life of obeying and serving God.

Please notice that this principle does not simply say *"obey."* It says *"obey immediately."* *Jam. 4:17* records an amazing insight into this process of obedience. James writes, *"Therefore, to him who knows to do good and does not do it, to him it is sin."* If you know what to do and fail to do it, even if you simply delay in doing it, James says it is sin. In other words, delayed obedience is simply another word for disobedience.

NOTES

What has God told you to do that you are not currently doing? Are you loving your wife as Christ loved the church? Have you forgiven those who have sinned against you? Have you confessed your sins and set your mind on heavenly things? Obey immediately! You are representing Jesus Christ as His messenger for this new church plant that will multiply other new churches. You have no option but to obey Him completely and immediately. Failure to obey immediately will hinder God's work in and through you. It will hurt your church. It will damage your ministry. Obey God immediately!

Assignment:

Much of this chapter was based on the story in *1 Sam. 3:1-21*. The three principles discussed on the last two pages were taken directly from an exposition of this passage. In fact, throughout this manual, I will be using various passages of the Bible not only to teach you but also to show you examples of proper exegesis and expositional sermons.

The three principles come directly from a sermon on *1 Samuel 3* that I have preached on "How to Hear God's Voice." Take the time to write my preaching outline in the space below. List under each of those three principles the verses that are used, illustrations that I included, as well as questions and applications.

Chapter 5
Preparing Our Hearts: Are You God's Man?

1. Introduction

Behind the content of the preacher is the character of the man. He must be set apart from worldly matters, be lifted above worldly aims and ambitions, and devoted above all else to God's service.

2 Chr. 16:9 says, *"For the eyes of the Lord run to and fro throughout the whole earth to show Himself strong on behalf of those whose heart is loyal to Him."* Another translation renders that last phrase, *"whose heart is completely His."*

How is your heart? To whom does it belong?

In this chapter we are going to look at what it means to prepare our hearts for preaching, to be fully and completely devoted to Him. We will discuss four dangers that lurk in the ministry that can make us slip and fall away from God.

2. Danger # 1 – Pursuing Head Knowledge Instead of Heart Knowledge.

I had the privilege of attending one of the finest seminaries in the world. I remember driving to that city to begin classes. I prayed that I would learn God's Word well and promised God that I would apply everything I learned to my life and ministry. My first class was in New Testament Greek, taught by a world-famous professor, Dr. Simon Kistemaker.

"Dr. K" had a unique way of teaching New Testament Greek. We were not allowed to bring anything into class except our Greek New Testament. Each day we would take a section of the Gospel of Mark, read it, learn vocabulary, and discuss all the nuances of grammar in that section. When it came time to take a test, He would simply assign the next chapter in that Gospel, and we were required to know everything about the words and grammar contained in that chapter.

Our first test was from *Mat. 4:1-20*. It is the famous Parable of the Sower, or the Farmer. I studied that passage for over forty hours. I worked hard and eventually knew everything I could possibly know about the Greek language in those verses. Finally, the night before the test, I was convinced I was ready. I set my books down and prepared to go to bed.

Shortly after laying down for the night, I realized something was horribly wrong. I had spent forty hours learning the Greek language, but never once did it even occur to me to ask the question, *"How is the soil of my heart? Am I receptive to God? Do I have fruitful soil?"* I had failed in the promise I made to God to apply everything I was learning to my life and ministry.

I got out of bed, knelt down and read those verses once again, this time out of my English Bible. And I prayed for God's forgiveness, and asked His Spirit to shine the light of His Word into the darkness of my heart and to make it good soil that would bear much fruit.

The next morning I awoke and went to class to take the test. As I remember, I received a good result. But what was more important was that I knew I had passed the real test before God.

Interestingly, after the test I told some of my fellow students about my experience and how I had failed to apply God's Word to my own life, even after forty hours of study. At that point, each of them admitted that they had done the same thing. It never even occurred to them to ask how the soil of their own lives was.

What about you? Has Bible study become only a head-knowledge exercise for you? I am not suggesting it is wrong to study the Bible. I am only suggesting that far too many of us stop at the point of "head-knowledge" and never make it to the point of "heart-knowledge."

That was the problem with the Pharisees in the first century. Jesus told these Bible scholars that they were mistaken, because they did not understand the Scriptures, or the power of God. They knew the Bible. They had memorized huge portions of the Old Testament. But they never applied it to their lives. May that never be true of us!

3. Danger # 2 – Busyness Rather Than True Devotion

A. Church planting is exciting. It is challenging. It requires a lot of energy. You will be stretched beyond your physical limitations with all there is to do to train leaders, do evangelism, meet needs, serve people, and lead the church. Preparing good sermons will require a lot of time. And the danger is that there will be little time for you to seek God. It is your responsibility – right now – to make a commitment to plan special times to seek the Lord.

B. One of my favorite stories in the Bible is found in *Luk. 10:38-42*. In fact, as I travel around the world and speak with church planters, I always find myself teaching from this passage. It's the story of Jesus coming to the house of Mary and Martha (and their brother Lazarus). There is a crowd of people seated there, listening to Jesus teach God's Word. Mary, one of the two sisters, was sitting right in front, at Jesus' feet, listening intently. And there was Martha, who was *"distracted, worried, and bothered"* about so many things that she could not even focus on what was going on.

Frustrated because of her excessive activity and the fact that her sister was not helping her, she finally complains to Jesus. She even accuses Him of not caring about her situation, and demands that He make Martha help her.

Jesus issues a loving and mild rebuke, saying gently, *"Martha, Martha, you are worried and troubled about so many things. But (only) one thing is needed, and Mary has chosen that good part, which will not be taken away from her." (10:41)*

His message to her was simple:
- Slow down. You are hurried and troubled in your life about so many things that you've forgotten the most important part. I am here with you. Learn from Me. My words to you are life. Take time to quiet your heart and regain perspective.
- Sit at His feet. That's what Mary had chosen to do. The house may have been dirty; the food may have been served late. But there was always time to clean house and cook food. Now was the time to be with Jesus and sit at His feet. In fact, Mary is seen three times *sitting at Jesus' feet*:
  ▶ She was sitting at the feet of Jesus to learn (*Luk. 10:39*). It was a picture of devotion.
  ▶ She was sitting at the feet of Jesus to receive help and comfort when her brother Lazarus had died (*Joh. 11:32*).
  ▶ She was sitting at the feet of Jesus to worship Him, anointing Him with oil (*Joh. 12:3*).

What about you? The focus of a disciple is his personal relationship with God. That comes first and foremost, before anything else. Activities and ministry involvements are the overflow of that relationship with God.

My brothers, this is a lesson that you will learn over and over in your life. You must come to the point where you identify with King Asaph's prayer in *Psa. 73:25-28*. Please take the time to memorize this passage. You will find yourself going back to its message many times in your church planting ministry.

Whom have I in heaven but you? And there is none upon earth that I desire besides You. My flesh and my heart fail, but God is the strength of my heart and my portion forever. For indeed, those who are far from You shall perish. You have destroyed all those who desert You for harlotry. But it is good for me to draw near to God. I have put my trust in the Lord God, that I may declare all Your works.

4. Danger # 3 – Losing Your First Love

Planting a church and seeing it multiply and plant other churches is a fantastic ministry. Researchers tell us there is no greater and effective way of doing evangelism than to plant reproducing churches. But it is possible to do all the right "things" and still miss out on what is most important.

That happened to a church in the first century. In fact, it was a church planted by the Apostle Paul, and pastored by his disciple Timothy. It was the only church in the New Testament to receive four letters that all made their way into the Bible. Do you know which one it was? It was the church at Ephesus. Paul wrote the first letter, Ephesians, to the entire church. He wrote two more to its pastor, 1 and 2 Timothy. And finally, Jesus Himself wrote a letter to this church in *Rev. 2:1-7*.

This church had a great beginning. It was strong in faith and love, and growing in hope (see *Eph. 1:15-18*). It was missionally minded, planting other churches throughout the region of Asia Minor. It held to a strong theology, sound doctrine and effective ministry. They persevered through many tough times. There was certainly a lot to celebrate about this church. In fact, there are eight very good qualities listed in *Rev. 2:2-3*.

That is why they must have been stunned when they received Jesus letter and read in *verse 4, "Nevertheless, I have this against you, that you have left your first love."*

Please notice, they did not *lose* their first love. They simply *left* it. The word means to misplace because of distraction. They were doing all the right things and forgot the most important thing: to love Jesus supremely.

Church planter, can you identify with this? Are you doing all the right things, but somehow your heart has grown cold toward Jesus? Have you misplaced your first love and become distracted by other things?

The solution is simple. True and good solutions are always simple because they always include a return to the basics. Jesus says three things to this church:

    A. Remember: the way it used to be when you loved Me with all your heart.

    B. Repent: confess your sin and turn back to God.

    C. Return: do the things you did at first. Return to the basics of your relationship with God. Seek God. Pray sincerely. Confess sin. Read the Word. Focus on Him.

> **Assignment**:
>
> Take a moment and do a "heart-inventory." Is Jesus truly your first love, or has that love relationship become misplaced, distracted by so many other things. Write out a prayer of repentance to God. Reaffirm your love and commitment to Him.

5. Danger # 4 – Falling Into Temptation

1 Cor. 10:12 is a great word to church planters: *"Therefore let him who thinks he stands take heed lest he fall."*

We can begin to think we are so strong that we could not possibly fall. Unfortunately the world is littered with Christian pastors and leaders who have thought this way. They have been blindsided by temptation and have dishonored the name of the Lord Jesus Christ.

Temptation is defined as follows: to try the strength of someone; to urge, to try to persuade, induce or entice, especially to something immoral or sensually pleasurable; to rouse desire in another person. Synonyms for temptation include: to bait, bribe, captivate, enchant, entice, lure, and snare.

Can you identify? A temptation is anything which seeks to persuade a Christian to sin against the Lord in any way and for any reason. The goal of every temptation is to cause an individual or group to sin. Without temptation, there would not be any incentive or desire within the individual to commit the sin. Temptation promises to repay the person with some type of pleasure for some type of disobedience.

To understand the context of this important verse, read the first twelve verses of *1 Cor. 10*. Notice in *verse 5* where it says that God was not pleased with *"most"* of them. That is a classic understatement, where God uses this to get our attention! Bible scholars have estimated that there were as many as one million people of Israel who escaped bondage from Egypt and wandered around in the desert for forty years. However only two of them (Joshua and Caleb) ultimately entered the Promised Land. The rest were *"laid low in the wilderness"* because of their sin.

1 Cor. 10:13 gives us hope and perspective:

> *No temptation has overtaken you except such as is common to man; but God is faithful who will not allow you to be tempted beyond what you are able; but with the temptation will also make the way of escape, that you may be able to bear it.*

From this one verse, I find seven principles that describe the truth about our temptations:

A. You are in dangerous territory when you think you can't fall (*10:12*). Watch out and be on the alert.

B. Your temptations seek to overtake you (*10:13a*). The picture of overtaking is one of a wrestler with a death-hold on his opponent.

C. Your temptations aren't unique to you, but are common to everyone (*10:13b*). They may seem larger than life, but the truth is that they are ordinary and common-place. We must unmask those temptations for what they really are: weak, limited and controllable.

D. God never abandons you in temptations due to His faithfulness (*10:13c*). See also *Psa. 33:4; Lam. 3:19-23; Psa. 145:13*. God's very character is on the line as He promises to aid us in the face of temptation.

E. God never permits any temptation to go beyond what you are able to endure (*10:13d*). Notice, God limits temptations according to His character. Because God is faithful, He is faithful to you personally. God not only provides salvation, He also provides protection from whatever temptation may seize you. He draws a line in the sand and decrees that a particular temptation may seize you only so hard, but no harder. It's because of His faithfulness that we may remain faithful to Him.

F. God always makes the way of escape in every situation. The language is very clear here: it is *the way of escape*. God provides that in each temptation. But we are responsible to choose that escape route.

NOTES

G. God limits every temptation so that you will be able to endure it. He provides the power for us to be able to endure through that temptation.

As a church planter, you will be tempted many times. Satan will seek to wreck your ministry, your marriage, your character and your testimony. You must remain strong. Remember the seven truths about temptation, and remain faithful to Jesus.

> **Assignment**:
>
> This chapter contains three passages of Scripture with outlines: *Luk. 10:38-42; Rev. 2:1-7; 1 Cor. 10:1-13.* Write them out here for future reference.

Chapter 6
Preparing Our Minds:
Do You Understand The Passage?

1. Introduction

In the previous two chapters, we have discussed two aspects of being prepared to preach. The first had to do with being called to preach. The second had to do with character and being God's man. Both of those are very important. But there is a third, and perhaps most important, aspect of preparation: understanding the passage we are to preach.

This book on Homiletics is the second of ten books to train church planters around the world. The first book, whose study you have already completed, dealt with Hermeneutics. The term *hermeneutics* is a big word for a simple but very important aspect of reading and teaching the Bible. It refers to the study of *interpreting* the Bible.

Dr. Earl Radmacher writes,

> *Hermeneutics is important because it helps us to avoid making mistakes in how we understand Scripture. This may at first seem like a strange idea. Why do we need help interpreting or explaining the words that we read? Do the words not speak for themselves? To understand why hermeneutics is important, imagine finding a letter that was written 100 years ago. You do not know who wrote it or why. You do not know the person to whom the letter is written. And you do not know the people, places, or even some of the words that it mentions. Now imagine you were asked to explain the letter to another person. You might be able to figure out some things, but you might make some wrong assumptions as well. In order to explain the letter correctly, you would need to know more about the author, the recipient, and the purpose of the letter.*
>
> *The Bible is the same. If we do not understand where the Bible came from, how it was written and why, we might make mistakes when we try to interpret it. Knowing this, hermeneutics provides us with the knowledge and skills we need to read the Bible, God's letter to us.*[13]

It is not my intention to repeat all the principles the previous book taught. Rather, I would like to build on its foundation and relate the subject of hermeneutics to homiletics.

2. The Bible Is The Ultimate Authority, Not The Preacher

The Bible refers to pastors as heralds of the message. In Biblical times, a *herald* was an individual who was sent out with news from the king. He would run from the palace to various cities and villages and would tell them the king's proclamation. In the same way, we have been given a message by our King, Jesus. He tells us to go all over the world and proclaim His message of salvation to cities, villages and people everywhere. We don't invent the message. We simply proclaim it.

A. The preacher is under the authority of the Bible just as those in the church.

B. The Bible judges the preacher and speaks to his soul as he prepares.

3. Proper Interpretation Is The Source For Effective Preaching

The Bible, properly interpreted and effectively taught, is powerful.

A. *"For the word of God is living and powerful, and sharper than any two-edged sword, piercing even to the division of soul and spirit, and of joints and marrow, and is a discerner of the thoughts and intents of the heart."* (*Heb. 4:12*)

B. *"And take...the sword of the Spirit, which is the word of God."* (*Eph. 6:17*)

C. *"And let the word of Christ dwell in you richly in all wisdom, teaching and admonishing one another in psalms and hymns and spiritual songs, singing with grace in your hearts to the Lord."* (*Col. 3:16*)

D. The longest chapter in the Bible is *Psalm 119*. Each of its 176 verses talks about the power of the Word of God and its relationship to us in our daily lives. Under the inspiration of the Spirit of God, David writes in verses *97-100:*

Oh, how I love Your law! It is my meditation all the day. You through your commandments make me wiser than my enemies, for they are ever with me. I have more insight than all my teachers, for Your testimonies are my meditation. I understand more than the ancients, because I keep Your precepts.

Please notice the concepts of wisdom, insight and understanding in this passage.
- In *verse 98*, the Word makes us wiser than our enemies. Wisdom from the Bible is superior to the knowledge we gain from experience.
- In *verse 99*, the Word gives us more insight than all our teachers. Insight from the Bible is more effective than knowledge gained from education.
- In *verse 100*, the Word causes us to have more understanding than the aged. Understanding from the Bible is greater than knowledge gained from years of living.

4. Faithful Preaching Depends On A Proper Understanding Of What God's Word Says

A. God works through His Word in the hearts of men and women.
"For as the rain comes down, and the snow from heaven, and do not return there, but water the earth, and make it bring forth and bud, that it may give seed to the sower and bread to the eater, so shall My word be that goes forth from My mouth; it shall not return to Me void, but it shall accomplish what I please, and it shall prosper in the thing for which I sent it." (*Isa 55:10-11*)

Assignment:

Select three of the following passages: Deu. 4:1; Psa. 19:7-10; 119:11, 105, 140; Isa. 34:16; Heb. 4:12. For each of the passages, read the passage and its immediate context; list those things from each verse that God's Word accomplishes in our lives.

Passage:

Passage:

Passage:

B. We must read the Word of God well and interpret it correctly.
"*Be diligent to present yourself approved to God, a worker who does not need to be ashamed, rightly dividing the word of truth.*" (2 Tim. 2:15) See also: *Deu. 17:19; Jos. 8:34; Mat. 22:29; 2 Pet. 1:19-21.*

C. There are many elements that contribute to understanding the true meaning of a text of Scripture.
  - The Holy Spirit helps us understand the Bible.
  - "*However, when He, the Spirit of truth, has come, He will guide you into all truth.*" (Joh. 16:13) See also: *2 Pet. 1:21; Luk. 24:45; Jam. 1:5.*
  - Scripture itself interprets Scripture. Clear passages in the Bible help us understand those passages that are more difficult to understand.
  - We learn the meaning of Scripture as we faithfully study the Bible.
    "*And these words which I command you today shall be in your heart. You shall teach them diligently to your children, and shall talk of them when you sit in your house, when you walk by the way, when you lie down, and when you rise up. You shall bind them as a sign on your hand, and they shall be as frontlets between your eyes. You shall write them on the doorposts of your house and on your gates.*" (Deu. 6:6-9) See also: *2 Tim. 3:14-15; Act. 17:11.*
  - The Holy Spirit speaks to us through other Christians.
    Then Philip opened his mouth, and beginning at this Scripture, preached Jesus to him (Act. 8:35). See also: *Luk. 24:32; 24:44-46; 1 Cor. 14:26.*
  - We learn the meaning of the Bible as we live out the teachings of the Bible.
    "*But be doers of the word, and not hearers only, deceiving yourselves. For if anyone is a hearer of the word and not a doer, he is like a man observing his natural face in a mirror; for he observes himself, goes away, and immediately forgets what kind of man he was. But he who looks into the perfect law of liberty and continues in it, and is not a forgetful hearer but a doer of the word, this one will be blessed in what he does.*" (Jam. 1:22-25) See also: *Psa. 1:1-3; Luk. 6:46-69.*

> NOTES

- We learn the meaning of the Bible as we use good rules of reading and study.
- We are helped in our understanding of the Bible as we use helpful tools of study (when they are available).

5. The Passage Determines The Message

A. The first task as we approach the Bible is to ask, *"What does this passage say? What does it mean?"* At this point you are performing the task of exegesis, which means to understand and explain the meaning of the text. *Exegesis* is the opposite of *Isogesis*, where you make the Bible say what you want it to say. We are not allowed to make the Bible say what we want it to say.

> *"For the time will come when they will not endure sound doctrine, but according to their own desires, because they have itching ears, they will heap up for themselves teachers; and they will turn their ears away from the truth, and be turned aside to fables."* (2 Tim. 4:3-4)

B. Draw principles from the text rather than reading into the text a message you hope or wish were there, but it really isn't.
- Remember, the Bible is the ultimate authority in your church plant. We must teach what it says, not what we wish it said.
- You are searching for the "Author's Intended Purpose." What did the author intend to communicate when he wrote that section of Scripture? We must preach the thought of the biblical writer.
- Remember that we are ultimately translators, taking the message that was written thousands of years ago in another language and to another culture, and proclaiming it in our language, to our culture, in our time.
- A good question to ask yourself when preparing to preach is: *Do I, as a preacher, make my thoughts match the Bible's thoughts – or do I change the Bible to make it match my own thoughts?* The sermon should always be an accurate reflection of what the Bible says.

6. Remember The Role Of The Holy Spirit As You Prepare And As You Preach

A. The Holy Spirit takes the Word of God to the people of God through the preacher of God to reveal the truth of God to accomplish the work of God in the church and the mission of God in the world.
- The Spirit teaches as we search the Scripture (*1 Pet. 1:10-12*).
- The Spirit convicts the world and glorifies Christ (*Joh.16:7-14*).
- The Spirit will not contradict the text (*Pro. 30:5-6*).
- The Spirit will enable us to see beyond the letter of the law to its true meaning (*Joh. 5:39-40*).

7. There Are Open Hand Doctrines And There Are Closed Hand Doctrines

A. All true Bible-believing Christians will agree on key doctrines, such as the deity of Christ, the inerrancy of the Word of God, and salvation by grace alone through faith alone in Christ alone. Those are doctrines that should be held with a closed hand. They are not up for negotiation.

B. There are other doctrines that are secondary in nature where true Christians disagree. Those doctrines are still important, but should be held with an open hand, and those who disagree with you should be treated with respect and honor.

8. Six Characteristics That Mark An Evangelical Interpretation Of The Bible

A. The Bible is to be read *privately*, by each individual, not a special ruling class of priests.

B. The Bible is to be read *rationally*, by understandable and practical reason. Ours is a rational faith.

C. The Bible is to be read *normally*, by reading it as you would any other book, not by viewing it as symbolic. The Bible was not meant to be understood by a select few. God wants everyone to understand His Word.

D. The Bible is to be read *systematically*, by expecting the Scripture to be consistent, complete, and self-explanatory, not the disorganized product of natural, cultural, and historical forces.

E. The Bible is to be read *prayerfully*, by expecting the Holy Spirit of Christ to guide the interpreter's heart, in addition to a systematic, academic approach.

F. The Bible is to be read with *Christ at the center*, by seeing each part as a contribution to an unfolding drama of redemption centered in the Gospel message.
- The Old Testament – the good news is coming.
- The Gospels – the good news is revealed.
- The Acts – the good news is spread.
- The Epistles – the good news is explained.
- The Revelation – the good news is fulfilled.

NOTES

Assignment:

Read each of these passages of the Bible and try to state the main concept (the one "Big Idea") that the author is trying to communicate.

John 1:1-14

Psalm 1:1-6

Genesis 22:1-19

Mark 4:35-41

Revelation 2:1-7

Now develop each of these passages into a sermon and preach these five messages to the new believers in your new church plant.

Chapter 7
Developing an Application-Centered Mindset

1. Introduction

True preaching speaks both to the head and the heart. But too often, preaching has become an intellectual exercise only. We must realize that the goal of preaching is not that we simply communicate Biblical information to people, but that we see that Biblical information transform their lives.

David prayed in *Psa. 119:11*: *"Your word I have hidden in my heart, that I might not sin against You."* He didn't say, Your word I have put in my pad of paper that it might look good with my other books!

2. The Difference Between an Exegetical and Homiletical Outline

A. As you study a passage of the Bible, it is often helpful to outline the author's flow of thought so you can more clearly understand what he is saying. This is what we would call an exegetical outline. It comes from the text itself and is used to show the meaning of a passage.

B. A homiletical, or preaching, outline is different. Though it is based on the text, it is directed toward the lives of those listening and is used to apply the meaning of a passage to people's lives.

C. Several years ago, I did a study of two famous American pastors and teachers, one near Los Angeles, California and another serving near Dallas, Texas. Both of these great men of God had preached through the Gospel of John. I ordered their study notes and was able to contrast how they approached the same passage. The passage I chose was *Joh. 14:25-31*.
- The first pastor's outline[14] was purely an exegetical one. The title of his sermon that day was *"What Jesus' Death Meant to Him."* It contained these four points:
  ▶ Jesus' Person Will Be Dignified (*14:28*).
  ▶ Jesus' Truth Will Be Documented (*14:29*).
  ▶ Jesus' Foe Will Be Defeated (*14:30*).
  ▶ Jesus' Love Will Be Demonstrated (*14:31*).
- His content was very good, Biblically focused and certainly doctrinally correct. But I was left with the sense that it did not connect with people's lives. There was no application other than *"we should know these truths."* He taught the Bible, but his teaching didn't change people's lives.
- The other preacher's outline[15] was clearly different. He spoke to people's needs. At the beginning of his sermon, entitled *"Overcoming Fear,"* he identified the fears people have and how those fears can affect their lives. Then he took his audience to the Scriptures for real-life answers. His outline was as follows: How is fear overcome?

> - By Depending on the Person of the Holy Spirit (*14:25-26*).
> - By Claiming the Peace of Jesus Christ (*14:27*).
> - By Accepting God's Plan for the Future (*14:28-29*).
> - By Following the Pattern of Obedience (*14:30-31*).

- This leader taught the same passage, with the same biblical content. But do you notice the difference? His message was directed toward the audience, it was targeted for application in people's lives, and it resulted in life-change.

D. Dr. Walter Kaiser is the former dean of Gordon Conwell Theological Seminary. He has written a book entitled *Toward an Exegetical Theology*, where he teaches this same idea.[16] He uses an example from a student's sermon on Balaam from *Num. 22:1-20*. The student's sermon outline was:
- Balaam Sought – *Num. 22:1-20*.
- Balaam Fought – *Num. 22:21-27*.
- Balaam Taught – *Num. 22:28-38*.

This outline has a cute rhyme to it in English, but not necessarily in other languages. I cannot imagine that anybody would show up to church on a Sunday morning with a passion to know what Balaam did. The focus on the sermon was not on his modern day audience, but on Balaam who lived many thousands of years ago. It gave content, but no relevant life-change. Both are needed!

The author then suggested a different approach. The focus he chose was on *"Knowing and Doing the Will of God,"* which is something that many people are concerned about today. He sought to show how Balaam did this by drawing out principles from the passage. He said, *"There are three ways in which we can know and do the will of God,"* and then had this as his outline:
- By Keeping the Faith – *Num. 22:1-7*.
- By Obeying God's Word – *Num. 22:8-22*.
- By Observing the Obstacles – *Num. 22:23-35*.

Notice how this outline remains true to the text but is oriented toward life today and application in the lives of its hearers. Though it teaches the passage, just like the exegetical outline did, it is directed toward application and relevance in the lives of the listeners.

Remember the homiletical focus:
- We don't just teach truth, we teach truth to transform people's lives!
- We don't just teach the Bible, we teach the Bible to people!
- We don't just teach content, we teach for life-change!

3. How Do We Focus on Application?

A. Ezra is a great example in the Old Testament. In *Ezr. 7:10* we read these words: *"For Ezra had prepared his heart to study the Law of the Lord, and to do it, and to teach statutes and ordinances in Israel."* Notice Ezra's three commitments:
- A commitment to study. You have already had a course on hermeneutics and have seen how important it is to correctly understand the meaning of the Biblical text.
- We see another example from Ezra's teaching, as recorded in *Neh. 8:8* where it says, *"They read from the book, the law of God, translating to give the sense so that they understood the reading."* It is critical that we understand what the text teaches.
- A commitment to obey. Ezra sought to obey what he read. You must be a doer of the word, not just a hearer only (*Jam.1:22-25*).
- A commitment to teach. Ezra must have had a burning desire, not only to know the Word of God for himself, but to make it known to others in his day, that they might also love the Lord their God with all their hearts.

B. I was studying the book of Deuteronomy and came across an interesting concept. The book of Deuteronomy contains a series of sermons given by Moses to the people of Israel shortly before going into the Promised Land. One of those sermons begins in *4:1* and says,

> *Now, O Israel, listen to the statutes and the judgments which **I teach** you to observe, that you may live, and go in and possess the land which the Lord God of your fathers is giving you.*

Chapter five begins Moses' next sermon to Israel with these words:

> *"And Moses called all Israel, and said to them, 'Hear, O Israel, the statutes and judgments which I speak in your hearing today, that you may **learn** them and be careful to observe them.'"*

I have highlighted two words in the verses above. In *4:1*, it is the word *teach*. In *5:1*, it is the word *learn*. In the Hebrew language, they are the same word, *lamad*. However, the author uses a different grammatical construction in each word that makes a significant difference in the meaning. The first word is a simple command. In *4:1*, Moses tells his audience they are to *teach* godly truths to the next generation. But when he begins the next sermon in chapter 5, the word *learn* is written in a way that implies that teaching carries with it a responsibility to cause others to learn the truths you are trying to teach them.[17]

In other words, teaching is causing someone to learn.

> **NOTES**

Now that may seem very simple, but I believe it is a revolutionary concept. Here are two significant implications:
- The Law of the Learner states: *the teacher has not fully taught until the student has fully learned!* It is not enough to be satisfied with presenting good content. We must continually ask ourselves the questions, *What are they doing with what I am saying? Are their lives any different because of what I have presented?* If not, you have not taught, biblically speaking.
- For the preacher, this means that your preaching is not effective until your listeners have understood what the Bible says, and are able to put into practice what it teaches. There are some who will disagree. They will say, *That's the role of the Holy Spirit. I am not responsible for what they do with the material I teach. I just need to be faithful to the Word of God.* But those people are wrong. God says the teacher is responsible to cause the student to learn.

4. How Important is Application?

It is important to have good, solid Biblical content. Our people must be taught the Word of God. But it is equally important that we spend time in each sermon showing people how these truths relate to their lives.

> *"All Scripture is given by inspiration of God, and is profitable for doctrine, for reproof, for correction, for instruction in righteousness, that the man of God may be complete, thoroughly equipped for every good work." (2 Tim. 3:16-17)*

Paul tells us four ways in which the word of God is profitable. Each begins with the Greek connective, *pros*, "for." It is profitable for (1) teaching and communicating doctrine, (2) reproof, or telling us where we have gone wrong, (3) correction, or putting us back on the right path, and (4) training in righteousness.

Writing about this passage, one scholar states:

> *Paul shows that the profit of Scripture relates to both creed and conduct. The false teachers divorced them; we must marry them....As for our creed, Scripture is profitable 'for teaching the truth and refuting error.' as for our conduct, it is profitable 'for reformation of manners and discipline in right living.' In each pair the negative and positive counterparts are combined. Do we hope, either in our own lives or in our teaching ministry, to overcome error and grow in truth, to overcome evil and grow in holiness? Then it is to Scripture that we must primarily turn, for Scripture is 'profitable' for these things.*[18]

2 Tim. 3:17 begins with the Greek word *hina*, translated by the phrase *in order that*. What is to be the end result of effective Bible teaching? It is completeness! The man of God is to be *adequately equipped for every good work*. To put it another way, the goal, then, is application, or life-change.

Did Paul do this in his writings? Did he impart knowledge in order to change lives? Absolutely! The letter to the Romans is the greatest doctrinal writing in all of the Bible. But did you ever realize how much of it is intended not for doctrine but for application? Let's take a look.

Rom. 1-5 and *9-11* are highly doctrinal. They are content-intensive. But *Rom. 6-8* and *12-16* are practical, or application-oriented. That means that 8 of the 16 chapters are devoted to content, and 8 are devoted to conduct. That is 50% doctrine, 50% application.

Let's take the book of Ephesians, Paul's great letter about the church. *Chapters 1-3* are primarily doctrinal, *chapters 4-6* are the application of that doctrine to their individual and corporate lives. Again, 50% doctrine, 50% application.

Colossians exhibits the same 50-50 balance, as do most of Paul's letters. The book of James is probably as high as 95% application-oriented; and Jesus' Sermon on the Mount equally as high.

If that was true of the letters of the New Testament (and what were those letters intended for but to be read aloud in the churches of the day), shouldn't our teaching reflect the same balance?

If you take the written sermons of Spurgeon, Luther, Calvin and others, you will see this same 50-50 balance. You'll also note this in many of the dynamic teachers of God's Word today. One study that we did in our master's program at *The International School of Theology* showed that popular pastor Chuck Swindoll averages 60% content, 40% application in his sermons.

Another evangelical scholar recently told the story[19] of teaching a 50-week elective course in the book of Romans at his church on Sunday evenings. He had labored over the great doctrines of man's sin, justification by faith alone, the eternal security of those who had been redeemed by the blood of Christ, the perseverance of the saints, etc.

During the progress of the course, the professor had been exposed to the evangelism training program, *Evangelism Explosion*. There he had learned the two "EE" questions:

> *If you were to die tonight, how sure are you that you would go to heaven?*
>
> *If God were to ask you, 'Why should I let you into my heaven?' what would you say?*

Those two questions are designed to diagnose what (or who!) people are trusting in for their salvation. This author decided to quiz his class on those two questions. After studying the great doctrines of Romans for over half a year, no one in that class could clearly articulate Biblical answers to the two "EE" questions. It was clear that though they had learned great truths, they had not incorporated those truths into their lives. It was head-knowledge, but not knowledge that had transformed their lives. As a result, they "failed" the test. Biblical teaching MUST be application-oriented.

A common trap Bible teachers fall into is to assume people can apply the Scripture themselves to their life situations. That is an assumption that we must not make. It's been my experience that the majority of people in our audiences don't actually think about what we are saying. It goes in the ear, through the body, down to the arm, where their hands write accurate notes. But somehow it still misses the mind! As Biblical communicators, we must make extra effort in showing how the Word of God applies to life.

NOTES

Another Bible teacher[20] tells the story of teaching this principle to a group of pastors. One was honest enough to admit that he was a "content only" type of guy, but was convicted about his need to balance content with application. He asked the teacher to pray for him that next Sunday as he spoke. This godly man said he would pray, and that he would call him that Monday to see how it went.

On Monday morning, the teacher dialed the pastor's number. "How did it go?" he asked enthusiastically?

"It was terrible," the pastor reported. "I usually speak for 40 minutes, so I decided I would share only 20 minutes of content. I tried all week long to think of applications, and I couldn't come up with any. So I just quit after 20 minutes. I could not think of one single application to what I was talking about."

With insight, he asked, "Did it ever occur to you that neither can the people in your audience?"

Pastors often take the easy way out at this point and add at the end of their sermons, "And now may God the Holy Spirit apply this teaching to our lives." Certainly the Spirit of God can and will do that, but it does not excuse the pastor and teacher from his responsibility of application.

I was thinking about this principle recently as I was preparing to speak at a student conference. They asked me to prepare note-taking outlines of my sessions so that those in the audience could follow along and take notes. I decided to include at the end of each session a series of "application points" specifically directed to their lives. At the evaluation session after the conference, that was one of the highest rated aspects of the entire conference. The common comment was "Now I know what to do as a result of what you have taught!"

If we are to be effective communicators, we must be application-oriented in our teaching and preaching.

Assignment:

Read the verses listed below and make a list of how you might teach each passage to your new church so they would know how to apply the Bible's teachings to their lives.

2 Timothy 3:16-17

Romans 6:1-14

Matthew 5:1-16

Joshua 1:1-9

Genesis 22:1-19

NOTES

Chapter 8
Developing your Homiletical Style

God has gifted you uniquely. You have a one-of-a-kind personality. There is no one like you! That means your style of preaching will also be unique. You possess gifts, abilities, personality and experience in ways that no one else does.

It is good to learn from others. It is not necessarily good to mimic their style. The way you exercise your preaching gifts through your own personality will be different from others. As you mature and gain preaching experience over the years, you will develop a style that is uniquely your own.

1. Choice # 1 – How Do I Approach The Bible?

Some choices regarding style are neither right nor wrong. They are simply reflective of your personality. However, the first decision you must make is a value-oriented decision. It relates to the way we approach the Word of God. I will refer to this choice as *"Exegesis or Isogesis."*

- A. *Exegesis* means to understand the meaning *out of* the passage. The one who exegetes Scripture seeks to determine its meaning and show his audience that meaning *from the text*. As one of my mentors used to say, *"You must keep your finger on the text!"* Your key objective is to determine what God has said.

- B. The opposite approach is *Isogesis*. This means you approach the Bible with a preconceived idea and read that meaning *into* the Bible. In its extreme case, the ideas of man become the authority and you are simply searching the Bible for proof-texts.

After taking the course in hermeneutics and reaching this point in our study of homiletics, I hope you see the wisdom in choosing an exegetical approach to preaching.

2. Choice # 2 – How Do I Approach My Preaching?

There are four good choices when it comes to our preaching style.

- A. <u>Preaching consecutively through books of the Bible</u>
  This is my preferred method of preaching, and I probably use this 60-75% of the time. I will choose a book of the Bible based on the needs of my congregation, outline it and preach a series of sermons that takes me from the beginning of the book all the way through till the end.

  There are several benefits to this style:
  - You preach the whole Word of God. You can't ignore one section of a book just because you don't like what it says.
  - It forces you to take each passage in the context of the whole book.
  - God delivered His truth to us in 66 books that had a unique purpose, con-

text and flow-of-thought. It seems that's the best way to present the Bible to others in our sermons.
- It makes you preach the entire Bible. This kind of preaching works through entire books of the Bible without skipping around. Even if dealing with one passage, it works to understand that passage and does not skip over its meaning.
- You will always have something to preach. The depths of God's Word can never be reached, so the preacher can never say that he has said all there is to say.

Let me give you several cautions and words of counsel as you preach consecutively through books of the Bible:
- Choose a book based on the needs of your congregation. Do they need a fresh view of Jesus? Choose one of the gospels. Do they need courage? Perhaps you might want to teach through the book of Daniel. Do they need to understand about the role of the church? Maybe Ephesians is the place to start.
- Don't get stuck. I know of a pastor who took eight years to preach through Matthew's gospel. That's way too long. I preached through Ephesians in twelve weeks – that's two weeks per chapter. That seemed to be a good pace. In preaching through longer books of the Bible (Hebrews, Gospels, Isaiah, etc.), I like to break them into smaller sections. One pastor I know taught John chapters 1-5, then did a short topical series, then came back and preached chapters 6-13, then interrupted that with another short series, and finally chapters 14-21.
- Work hard at being applicationally-driven in your sermons.
- Make sure you remind your congregation of the big picture of the book. It's easy to forget that over several months.

B. Topical Series

There are times when it is appropriate to present a topical series of messages. Perhaps you want to talk about what God says about marriage, parenting, spiritual gifts, the purpose of the church, or how to know God's will. Other times you might want to address specific doctrines like salvation, sanctification, what God is like, or spiritual warfare.

Topical series can be very practical, very focused toward specific needs or areas of instruction, and very beneficial to your audience.

Here are some principles about preaching topical sermons effectively in your new church plant:
- Topical series are often used to meet specific needs in the congregation. Perhaps your church members are facing hard times. You might consider presenting a series on faith from the Gospels. Maybe they need a challenge to become mission-minded and begin planting churches. You could do a series on church planting from the book of Acts.
- It is possible to base your topical sermon on a passage of Scripture. If you are discussing marriage, perhaps it is *Ephesians 5:22-33*. If it is spiritual gifts, perhaps *1 Corinthians 12*. In doing this, you are actually able to present an expository message, teaching one passage of Scripture per sermon.

- Be careful of falling into the trap of proof-texting with Bible verses taken out of context.
- One form of topical sermons is a biography. I've done a twelve-week series on the life of Abraham, primarily taken from *Genesis 12-22*. I've also done a series on the great prophets, talking about one prophet each week.
- A doctrinal series can challenge your church toward greater depth in their understanding of the Word of God.
- I have occasionally taught a series on Apologetics (reasons why Christianity is true), and answers to tough questions.
- My encouragement would be to preach through books of the Bible as your normal habit, and intersperse that with shorter, topical series.

C. <u>A Preaching Calendar</u>
Some church traditions actually set up a yearly calendar of topics for their preachers to follow. Though I do not generally like this approach, there are certain times when the calendar does help dictate our messages. Consider:
- Christmas. Every year I will do at least one Christmas message. Sometimes I will do a series of 3 or 4 Christmas messages.
- Easter. What a great time to do a message on the resurrection, or possibly a series on what the death, burial and resurrection of Jesus means to us.
- Special events and holidays. In the United States, we celebrate "Labor Day" the first Monday in September. That weekend I will often do a special sermon on God's view of work. What are the unique holidays your culture has? What Biblical truths would be appropriate to teach at those times?
- Perhaps you have a yearly missions conference at your church. You might consider a four-week series on the Great Commission leading up to that conference.

D. <u>Evangelistic Sermons</u>
Though all sermons should point toward Christ, there are some that are specifically focused on a clear presentation of the Gospel for unbelievers.

- Evangelistic exposition is preaching with the specific goal of calling lost people to trust in Christ.
- It is God's desire that people come to Christ and receive salvation through our preaching.
- Some passages lend themselves very naturally to evangelistic preach. *Romans 10:9-10*, for example, lead to a clear and passionate offer of the Gospel to lost people. Many of the miracles of Jesus point to who He is and what He has done.

E. <u>The Shot-Gun Approach</u>
I said earlier that there were four valid styles and approaches in preaching. This is not one of them! The Shot-Gun approach has many weaknesses. This approach pulls Bible verses from everywhere, many times taking those verses out of context. We need to be very careful with an approach such as this. Remember my professor's advice: *Keep your finger on the text!*

Assignment:

Read *2 Corinthians 5:14-21*.

What is the "big idea" in these verses? What is the message you would want to communicate to your church from these verses?
Develop an outline from these verses. Your outline may have 3 points, maybe more or less…it could have one main point. Simply leave blank any extra points or add points as needed. Feel free to add sub-points beneath your main points.

Big Idea:

Point 1

Point 2

Point 3

Now take a second passage, *1 Corinthians 13*, and do the same thing.

Big Idea:

Point 1

Point 2

Point 3

Finally, take a third passage, *1 Thessalonians 1*, and do the same thing.

Big Idea:

Point 1

Point 2

Point 3

Chapter 9
The Big Idea

1. Introduction

Here's a practical assignment: several days after preaching a sermon, ask ten people who were there to tell you what you talked about. Can they remember your main text? What about the 3 or 4 points you made? Can they remember those? What about the sermon title, can they even remember that?

I've done that assignment, and it's humbling to have spent 20 hours preparing a great sermon and have no one remember it three days later.

I am not advocating people memorize your sermon outlines. But it would be nice if they could at least remember something!

One of the ways to help people remember is to center your sermon around one big idea. A big idea is a short phrase or sentence that is memorable and accurately summarizes the one thing you want people to remember.

Two weeks ago I heard a friend of mine preach a sermon on *Genesis 6:1-10*. It is the introduction to the story of Noah and God's decision to send the flood to judge mankind. The last phrase of *verse 5* describes mankind's hearts: *"every intent of the thoughts of his heart was only evil continually"*.

The last three words of that verse served as my friend's "Big Idea": Only evil continually. He repeated that phrase a dozen times throughout his sermon. And two weeks later, I still remember it: the heart of man is sinful. We do *"only evil continually,"* and are in desperate need of a Savior.

The marks of a good big idea are (1) that it is true to the Biblical text; and (2) that people can remember it and see how it relates to their lives. *"Only evil continually"* truly summarizes the intent of the passage, and it is memorable and relevant to our lives. Several weeks later, I can still remember that statement, and God is still using it in my life.

Assignment:

In the last chapter, you wrote a Big Idea and a preaching outline from *2 Corinthians 5:14-21*. What was your big idea? Was it memorable? Did it adequately and accurately summarize the one thing you wanted people to remember from your sermon? Discuss this with your fellow church planters.

2. Big Ideas Should Be Memorable

A. Spend the time during your sermon preparation to identify a big idea that is worth remembering.

B. Make it short and concise. You should be able to express the main idea in one, clear phrase or sentence.

C. Repeat the big idea frequently throughout the sermon.

D. Encourage them to remember the big idea. You might even have them say it out loud with you.

3. Big Ideas Should Be Biblical

A. Make sure it accurately reflects the meaning of the passage.

B. Your big idea should be evident from the text.

C. Consider using the words of the text itself in your big idea.

4. Big Ideas Should Be Significant

A. The Bible contains many life-changing ideas.

B. Your big idea must have substance.

5. Big Ideas Should Be Directed Toward Your Audience

A. What is it that God is saying to your people through this passage of Scripture?

B. How will this truth change the people who embrace it? Why is it important to them?

6. Developing the Big Idea

One leader who has taught preaching all around the world to pastors and church planters[21] suggests three questions that deal with the meaning, validity and the implications of any idea. The questions should be addressed not only to the big idea but to the supporting ideas and the details of the passage as well. This helps you decide what kind of supporting material you will need to communicate the message of the text.

A. What does this mean? What has to be explained so that the listeners in my new work will understand the passage?
  - Does the biblical writer explain his statements or define his terms? Does he assume that the original readers understood him and needed no explanation?
  - Are there concepts, terms or connections that modern listeners might not understand that you need to explain to them?

B. Is this true? Do I really believe it? What needs to be proved?
- Is the author arguing, proving or defending at length some concept that your hearers would probably accept? Examples might be that Jesus was human or that Christians do not have to be circumcised.
- Is the author arguing, proving, or defending a concept that your listeners may not readily accept, and therefore need to understand the argument of the passage? For example, that slaves were to be obedient to their masters.
- Is the author assuming the validity of an idea that your listeners may not accept right away? Do they need to be convinced what the passage asserts is actually the case? For instance, that Jesus is the only way to God, or that the Bible is unique and contains the very breath of God.

C. So what? What difference does it make? How should this concept be applied?

One of the best ways to understand how to include applications in your sermons is to make sure you are applying these truths to your life. If you are in the habit of applying Scripture to your life on a daily basis, it will be easier for you to include good applications in your sermons.

It is helpful to me to listen regularly to the people to whom I am ministering. What are their hurts? What are their joys? What are their needs? Where are they struggling? What misconceptions do they have about God's character? What sins are they battling? When I know the answers to those questions, application points become easy.

7. Examples of Big Ideas

A. One leader preached a sermon on *Exodus 13:17-18*. His big idea was "The shortest distance between two points may be a zig-zag."

B. I recently heard one communicator teach from *Romans 12:1-7*. His big idea was "When the effect of the gospel is all-important in the church, the force of the gospel is unstoppable in the world."

C. In preaching *Romans 2:1-19*, the big idea might be "If you use the law as your ladder to heaven, you will be left standing in hell."

D. From *Romans 6:1-14*, the big idea could be, "Through their union with Jesus Christ, Christians have died to the rule of sin and are alive to holiness." However, a more striking statement might be, "You are not the person you used to be; therefore, don't handle life as you used to handle it."

E. The central lesson from the parable of the Good Samaritan in Luke *10:25-37* might be, "Your neighbor is anyone whose need you see, whose need you are in a position to meet."

8. Suggestions for Writing the Big Idea

> NOTES

A. State the idea as simply and as memorably as possible. Make each word count.

B. State the idea in clear and familiar words. If you were given one sentence in which to communicate your idea to someone who didn't know religious words and who couldn't write it down, how would you say it?

C. State the idea so that it focuses on response. How do you want your listeners to respond? Instead of "You can rejoice in trials because they lead to maturity," say, "Rejoice when the hard times come." If you know what your listeners should do, tell them!

D. State the idea so that your listeners sense you are talking to them about them.

Assignment:

Read the following passages. Write down a "Big Idea" from each one.

Isaiah 6:1-8

Mark 4:35-41

Ephesians 2:8-9

Colossians 3:1-4

Psalm 27

> NOTES

Chapter 10
Sermon Points That Make a Point [22]

1. Introduction

In chapter 7, we discussed developing an application-centered mindset. I would like to go one step further and help you learn how to build an outline that is application centered.

It's been my experience that books on preaching lift up the wrong kind of sermons as examples. They tend to teach you to prepare academic outlines that are so vague and general that they are robbed of power.

For instance, here's an outline for a sermon based on *1 Corinthians 12*, "The Corinthians and Spiritual Gifts" (By the way, that title probably does not make most people want to listen).

    A. Point #1: The source of the Corinthians' gifts.

    B. Point #2: The function of the Corinthians' gifts.

    C. Point #3: The purpose of the Corinthians' gifts.

    Here is what I think is wrong with this outline:
- It is general and not very specific. It suggests an academic outline rather than a plain explanation of Biblical application.
- It is written in the third person, and therefore, not personal at all. It's about somebody else, the Corinthians, not your current audience.
- It's in the past tense, which gives the impression *"that was then and this is now."*
- It doesn't mention either God or people. Do you really have a great sermon if you don't mention either God or people?

    D. In short, the points don't say much of anything to anyone. You can avoid this by taking a few simple steps toward creating points that make a point.

2. Use The Biblical Application As the Points Of Your Sermon

    A. Most sermons look like this:
- Point #1 describing the text.
- Point #2 describing the text.
- Point #3 describing the text, followed by an application section.

    Or like this:
- Point #1 describing the text, then application.
- Point #2 describing the text, then application.
- Point #3 describing the text, then application.
- Point #4 describing the text, then application.

B. I want to suggest a third alternative that reverses this process. Start with the application in your own setting and show how the Scripture illustrates it. It looks something like this:
- A present tense application statement for your first point and then the content of the text.
- A present tense application statement and then the content of the text.
- A present tense application statement and then the content of the text.

This outline gets the Biblical application right out in front, stating the application as the sermon point rather than saving the application for the end of the sermon.

3. Put Action In Every One Of Your Sermon Points

A. The easiest way to help people be doers of the Word is to put action in the point. It turns the biblical truth into action steps. For instance, I once did a message from *1 Corinthians 13* on *Building Loving Relationships in a Loveless World*. The points of the message were:
- Accept people just the way they are.
- Believe they are valuable.
- Care when they hurt.
- Desire what is best for them.
- Erase all past offenses.

I ended the sermon by pointing to Jesus and showing how He does each of those things for us. He accepts us just the way we are (we don't have to change or improve in order for Him to love us). He believes we are valuable (created in His image). He cares when we hurt. He desires what is best for us. His death on the cross has paid for our sins and extends the gracious offer of erasing all our offenses (past, present and future). The outline contains five Biblically-based points, all of the application statements with action. By the end of the sermon, every person had something they could go back and put into practice in their daily lives.

I've actually preached that sermon all around the world, with great response.

4. Place The Words "Jesus" Or "God" Into Each Of Your Points

I'm very concerned about pastors who try to build messages based on solely reaching unbelievers by eliminating "God" and "Jesus" from the message. In fact, I think the best sermons put "God" or "Jesus" right into the applications points. When you stand to preach, you're not just giving a moralistic talk. You want to change lives, and the power for changed lives comes only from God.

I think one of the reasons some pastors aren't preaching passionately in new church plants today is because their points aren't passionate points. But you'll develop a passion for the points when you start talking about what God can do in someone's life.

When we leave God out of a sermon (and the sermon outline), and talk only about what we must do, then we encourage self-confidence in our listeners as opposed to God-confidence. By focusing on God, you'll encourage your congregation to develop trust and faith in Him alone.

5. Personalize Your Sermon Points By Using Personal Pronouns

A. I rarely use the word "we" in an application or an outline because it weakens the application. In other words, say, "Jesus Christ came for me. Jesus Christ died for me. Jesus Christ is coming again for me." It's more personalized.

B. The academic outline cited above (*1 Cor. 12*) looks radically different when it becomes personalized. Compare the difference when the same message changes from "The Corinthians and Spiritual Gifts" to "Using Your Gifts."
- Point #1 – God gave you gifts.
- Point #2 – God gave you gifts to use.
- Point #3 – God gives you gifts to use for the benefit of the body.

Assignment:

Before I give you my feedback, do you like this outline better than the previous, academic one? Why or why not?

Why do I like this outline better? There are at least four reasons:
- It's personal.
- It's practical.
- It's God-centered.
- It's positive.

---

6. During Your Sermon Suggest A Practical Assignment For The Week

I often assign some homework! This reflects the way Jesus taught. He often gave assignments by saying, "Go and do likewise."

Once a pastor on the West Coast of the United States was doing a two-week series on finances, the homework assignment for the congregation was to write out a practical budget for the year. They gave people some tools at the end of the worship service, and then over the next two Wednesday nights offered a short workshop that taught them how to handle their finances, based on the Biblical messages they'd been hearing on Sunday.

It's not enough just to give people God's principles in getting out of debt; you need to show them how and what to do by giving practical, follow-up applications.

Good, Biblical applications have five characteristics:

A. They are specific. The words "more" and "less" are not specific enough. Instead of saying "I am going to pray more," you need to say, "I am going to pray every day for 30 minutes for myself, my family and my new church work." That is a specific application.

B. They are motivational. Does the assignment motivate people to action and change? If it is not motivating, don't even suggest it. Otherwise, they won't do it anyway.

C. They are attainable. Don't give assignments that are unrealistic; that will just discourage them. Instead, phrase your applications in ways that people will respond, "I see how I can do that in my life."

D. They are relevant to people's lives.

E. They can be measured. Does it allow people to measure their progress?

Assignment:

In chapter 7 you wrote out a preaching outline from *2 Corinthians 5:14-21*. By design, I had you work on that before teaching you about sermon points that make a point.

Now, take the outline you developed earlier and make improvements to it based on what you learned in this chapter.

Big Idea:

Point 1

Point 2

Point 3

Chapter 11
Introductions, Conclusions and Illustrations

1. Introductions

I was listening to a friend of mine teach about missions and the need to be actively involved in making a difference in the world. Here is how he began his excellent sermon on the subject of Activism:

> *The other day I was reading the newspaper and an article caught my attention. It was about two elderly ladies in West Virginia in the United States. A bookstore (that sold pornographic material) moved into their community. Well, the two elderly ladies took offense at that, so they went to the proprietor and asked him very kindly if he would consider moving his bookstore to another place. The response, they said in the article, was "not favorable." So they decided to go to the mayor and present their case. The mayor said he certainly empathized with them, but there was simply nothing he could do. So they took the situation into their own hands. Each of them grabbed a camera and stood outside of the bookstore and during the opening hours of the store, took pictures of everyone who came out. After three months, the bookstore was closed down and the owner agreed to move to a different county. The thing I loved about the article is that at the end, one of the ladies mentioned, almost as an aside, "You know, we didn't even have film in the camera." Isn't there something very refreshing about individuals who are so burdened by an issue of their times, that they take action. Tonight, we are going to take a look at the lost art of activism.*

That's a good introduction. It captures our attention, it introduces the subject, and it motivates the audience to listen.

A. The Introduction is a very important part of your sermon, and the most often overlooked. You only have a few minutes to gain their attention, and to get them to focus on you and your presentation. I recently used this quote when beginning a sermon on living fully devoted to the Lord Jesus Christ:

> *A great Scottish preacher once said, "If we could only show the world that Christianity is not a boring religion, but the greatest adventure the human spirit can know, then those people who have been standing outside our churches looking at us as if we were crazy, would come crowding in, and we would see the greatest revival since Pentecost!"*

B. A good introduction will motivate your audience to listen to you. One preaching professor has said that the goal of giving a speech is to keep the audience awake for 45 minutes. I put it this way: to speak without first gaining attention is like talking on the telephone before the other person has answered the phone.

C. A good introduction will introduce the topic of your message and will help your audience understand the organization of the rest of the sermon.

D. An Example of a Good Introduction:
The following introduction is from a sermon I preached from *1 Corinthians 10* entitled *The Truth about Temptations*.

> *One of my favorite memories from my childhood is going fishing with dad. I always looked forward to it because I loved being with my dad. I remember the first time he ever took me fishing. We arrived at my dad's favorite spot, and he pulled out a bucket of live bait. There were worms and other moving bugs and insects. It wasn't very attractive, at least to me. I remember asking my dad, "Why are we using this terrible stuff? It stinks!" And my dad very calmly said, "It may not be attractive to you, but it is to a fish!*
>
> *The purpose of bait is to lure and tempt the fish into biting it. The problem, for the fish, is that the bait contains a hook, a hook that will ultimately result in the death of the fish.*
>
> *What causes a person who is walking with Jesus to become unholy? Sin! And what causes a person to sin? It is temptation. Just like that poor fish is tempted to bite the bait, we are tempted to take the bait of sin, and when we do, the results are not good for us, just like they weren't good for the fish my dad and I caught.*
>
> *What is temptation? A temptation is anything which seeks to entice us to sin against the Lord in any way and for any reason. The goal of every temptation is to cause us to sin. Temptation promises to repay the person with some type of pleasure for some type of disobedience.*
>
> *Therefore the key to personal holiness is to experience personal victory over temptation. How do we do that? There is a passage in the Bible that speaks directly to the subject of experiencing victory over temptation. Turn in your Bibles to 1 Corinthians 10:1-13.*

Assignment:

What makes this a good illustration? Why?

2. Conclusions

There are four functions of a conclusion:

A. It tells them you're about to stop your message.

B. It summarizes the main points.

H. Grady Davis, in his book *Design for Preaching*, wrote:

The conclusion is the moment in which listeners can come nearest to seeing the idea whole and all at one time. It is the moment in which the issue can be seen at its clearest, felt at its sharpest, and carried back into life where, if anywhere, it must be resolved. The conclusion is the last chance to accomplish the speech's purpose, whatever that may be. [23]

C. It specifies a desired response.
- Affirmation: keep doing something.
- Prevention: don't do something.
- Motivation: begin doing something.
- Discontinuance: stop doing something.

D. It ends on a powerful note.

I encourage you to write out your conclusion word for word. Even great and accomplished speakers have felt it necessary to write down and all but memorize the exact words of their closings.

3. Illustrations

Illustrations are powerful. They speak strongly to people all around the world. I've spoken in Asia, Africa, Europe and the Americas. Everywhere I go, people respond to stories and illustrations. What is it about illustrations that speak so strongly to us? It is their ability to hold our attention, because they add color and feeling to a presentation.

Four Purposes of Illustrations:

A. Illustrations make the meaning clear. The Roman statesmen and philosopher, Seneca, said: Rules make the learner's path long; examples make it short and successful.

B. Illustrations help listeners remember. Jesus often used illustrations. He talked about the lamp under the bushel, the city on top of the hill, the camel and the eye of the needle. His listeners were familiar with every one of those images.

C. Illustrations allow repetition without weariness. They show a fit with life and reinforce the truth.

D. Illustrations sustain interest and keep people motivated to listen to you.

E. Illustrations move the emotions. Stories, analogies and visual pictures appeal to our emotions.

Illustrations are like windows that let in light to a room. Illustrations brighten our presentations and help people to see clearly what we are talking about.

Assignment:

Listen to a sermon by a fellow pastor or church planter. Pay special attention to their introduction, conclusion and illustrations.

What did they do well?

How could they improve in the future?

What changes do you need to make in your style to have good introductions, conclusions and illustrations?

Chapter 12
Outlining and Organizing

At this point in your message preparation, you should know what the big idea is that you have to preach and why you are preaching it. Now the question is: What shape will the sermon take? What is the best approach to convey this message?

1. Purposes Of An Outline

There are many ways of outlining a sermon. An outline helps you organize and structure a sermon. It allows your audience to follow you more carefully. And it helps you as a communicator to stay focused and on track as you deliver the sermon.

2. Suggestions For Outlining

A. Keep your outline simple and easy for your listeners to follow.

B. Most effective outlines have 3-7 points. If you have any more than seven points, it becomes difficult for your audience to remember. (Twenty years ago I sat through a sermon by Dr. Bill Bright where he used 36 points in a sermon from *Colossians 3*. I don't remember a single thing he said ... other than there were 36 points in his message!)

C. Keep your points parallel to each other and equal in structure.

D. Make sure that your audience can see where these points come from in the text.

3. Examples Of Outlines

A. <u>The Application-Based Outline</u>
In chapter ten we discussed this method, and said it looks something like this:
- A present tense application statement and then the content of the text.
- A present tense application statement and then the content of the text.
- A present tense application statement and then the content of the text.

B. <u>An Idea to Be Explained</u>
One of Europe's finest preachers prepared this outline from *Colossians 1:15-18*.
- The relation of Christ to God is that He is, *"the image of the invisible God"* (1:15).
- The relation of Christ to creation is that He is, *"the firstborn of all creation"* (1:15-17).
- The relation of Christ to His church is that He is, *"the head of the body,"* who is *"the beginning, the firstborn from the dead"* (1:18).

C. A Idea to be Proved
In *1 Corinthians 15:12-19*, Paul argues for the resurrection of the body. The big idea is *"The Christian faith is worthless unless Christians rise from the dead."* In outline form the sermon would look like this:
- If Christians do not rise, the Christian faith lacks valid content (*15:12-14*).
- If Christians do not rise, the apostles are despicable liars (*15:15*).
- If Christians do not rise, then the Christian faith is useless (*15:16-17*).
- If Christians do not rise, then Christians have no hope (*15:18-19*).

D. The Whiting Method
This method, named after a respected preacher and trainer of preachers, seeks to follow the outline of the text and uses a format of *"explain, illustrate and apply"* under each main point. A sermon from *John 15:1-27* entitled "Three Priorities of Every Believer" will look like this:
- Priority #1 – Abiding in Christ (*1-11*).
  - ▶ Explain the Principle.
  - ▶ Illustrate the Principle.
  - ▶ Apply the Principle.
- Priority #2 – Loving one Another (*12-17*).
  - ▶ Explain the Principle.
  - ▶ Illustrate the Principle.
  - ▶ Apply the Principle.
- Priority #3 – Witnessing to the World (*18-27*).
  - ▶ Explain the Principle.
  - ▶ Illustrate the Principle.
  - ▶ Apply the Principle.

E. The Geographical Method
The Lead Pastor of one of the world's largest evangelical churches recently preached a series from the life of Elijah. This sermon, entitled "When You're Running Out of Everything," was taken from *1 Kings 17:1-16*. Notice it works through the three geographical places in which Elijah found himself:
- At The Brook Cherith: The Ravine of Obscurity. Three Reasons God allows the brook to dry up:
  - ▶ To keep me from depending on the brook instead of God.
  - ▶ To move me to a better place.
  - ▶ To prove God hasn't forgotten me.
- The Journey North: The Road of Insecurity. What to remember:
  - ▶ The path to a miracle is always through uncomfortable territory.
  - ▶ The source of a miracle is always unexpected.
  - ▶ The pattern for a miracle is always Command-Promise-Risk.
- Zarapeth: The Refinery of Scarcity. What to remember in times of scarcity:
  - ▶ Whatever I need more of; I give all I have of it to God.
  - ▶ Whatever I have the least of, I give back to God.
  - ▶ I don't give to get a blessing. I give to be a blessing.

- Summary: Lessons for Troubled Times:
  ▶ God is all I need.
  ▶ Where God guides, He provides – His direction is His provision.
  ▶ I must trust Him one day at a time.
  ▶ God's promises hinge on my obedience.

"My God will meet all your needs according to his glorious riches in Christ Jesus" Philippians 4:19.

F. <u>A Story Told</u>
The Bible is a book of stories. Old Testament theology comes packaged in narratives of men and women who go running off to set up their handmade gods and of others who take God seriously enough to live their lives for Him.

When Jesus appeared, He came telling stories.

The details of a story are woven together to make a point, and all the points develop the central idea of the sermon.

There are many other forms sermons can take. I use many different styles, so that I won't fall into a habit and become predictable in my preaching style.

At the end of this book, I am including outlines from preachers and teachers around the world. Their style reflects their personality, training, culture, audience and experience. Learn from them, but be careful not to copy them. You must ultimately develop your own style based on your gifting, personality, training, culture, audience and experience.

4. Editing Your Sermon

I'm like many other preachers. I like to preach long messages! But sometimes "less is more." Jesus' most famous sermon, The Sermon on the Mount (*Matthew 5-7*) takes only 20 minutes to read out loud.

Every preacher needs to learn to trim his sermons. If you use everything you learn in a week of studying, you'll have to preach all day!

When I set out to trim my sermons after a long week of studying, I trim in four places:

A. Number of verses: To really understand what God's Word says about what I'm preaching, I have to study as many verses as possible. But there's no way I can use all those verses as I preach. That means I must edit, trim and focus on what is really important for my message. I admit this is tough for me. I hate to trim verses. The danger for us preachers is to try to communicate *everything* we have studied. You can't do that.

B. Background material: I hate to tell you this, but your church members aren't nearly as fascinated by archeology and linguistics as you are. Do as much background study as you can in the exegesis, but share as little of it as possible in your sermon. Remember, preaching is not a seminary class. You are preaching for life change. You don't have to explain everything about a text to your congregation. Describing too much detail of the text can actually hide or dilute the power of the text. When you pay too much attention to secondary issues, you miss the point and purpose of the verse. Figure out the purpose of the text and emphasize that.

C. Points: The Puritan preachers would often use 30, 40, or 50 points in their sermons. But exhaustive sermons are exhausting to the congregation. Here is a principle of life: confinement often produces power. When an artist confines his painting to a canvas, a picture comes out. When water is confined to one channel, it produces hydroelectric power. When pianists confine their playing to the score, music is produced. When you confine your sermons to fewer points, you get a sermon with power.

D. Quotes and illustrations: You've got to trim your illustrations too. Often we spend way too much time telling a story. Don't draw out your stories; condense them. A good story becomes a great story when you use as few of words as possible. Take a look at all of your stories. Can they be any shorter?
- Also, don't forget to take a look at your quotes. Sometimes you will find an archaic quote that has a good idea in it. Well, just rephrase it. Shorten it to give it power. You can also look at limiting the number of quotes or outside illustrations you're using if your message is too long.

You might as well face it now. You're going to have to trim your sermon at some point this week. In fact, no matter how long it is, ask yourself one question: Can it be better?

Look at limiting your verses, cutting background material, taking out points, and trimming your quotes and illustrations. The result will be a sermon that has more focus and therefore it will have more power.

Assignment:

Choose a recent sermon. What was your outline? Write it out in the space below.

Knowing what you now know, edit your outline to make it more effective.

NOTES

Chapter 13
The Role of the Holy Spirit in Preaching

1. The Role of the Holy Spirit in Relationship to the Preacher

The Holy Spirit must be at work in the life of the preacher. There are primarily three of His ministries that are relevant here: illumination, guiding and empowering.

    A. <u>Illumination</u>
It is impossible to properly understand the Word of God apart from the light the Spirit of God sheds on it. Illumination is not equated with either revelation or inspiration. It communicates no new divine truth, but rather enables us to <u>understand</u> God's truth in the Bible. No clear understanding of Scripture leading to powerful preaching is possible without the Spirit's work of illumination.[24]

David prayed: *"Open my eyes, that I may see wondrous things from Your law." (Psa. 119:18)* That should be the prayer of each believer, but especially the preacher.

"Teach me, O Lord, the way of Your statutes, and I shall keep it to the end. Give me understanding, and I shall keep Your law. Indeed, I shall observe it with my whole heart." (Psa. 119:33-34) The Holy Spirit of God must teach us. Spiritual truth is spiritually discerned.

After the resurrection, on the road to Emmaus, Jesus *"opened their understanding, that they might comprehend the Scripture."(Luk. 24:45)* That is exactly what we need Him to do as we study in preparation for our sermons.

Paul prayed for the believers at Ephesus, saying: *"that the God of our Lord Jesus Christ, the Father of glory, may give to you the spirit of wisdom and revelation in the knowledge of Him, the eyes of your understanding being enlightened; that you may know what is the hope of His calling, what are the riches of His inheritance in the saints." (Eph. 1:17-18)* I often ask people to pray those verses for me as I prepare to speak.

    B. <u>Guidance</u>
We must trust God to guide us in our preparation and sermon delivery. In *Luk. 4:1*, we read that Jesus, *"being filled with the Holy Spirit, returned from the Jordan and was led by the Spirit into the wilderness."* Even Jesus did nothing on His own initiative, but only as He was led by the Father *(Joh. 5:30)*.

Jesus taught that the Spirit would play a vital role in the life of each believer. In *Joh. 7:37-39*, Jesus said, *"If anyone thirsts, let him come to Me and drink. He who believes in Me, as the Scripture has said, out of his heart will flow rivers of living water. But this He spoke concerning the Spirit, whom those believing in Him would receive."* God the Holy Spirit will guide us and produce through us a quality of life that will be refreshing and attractive.

Jesus promised that the Spirit would teach the disciples all things and bring to their remembrance all that He said to them (*Joh. 14:26*).

The Spirit would also guide the disciples into all truth, speaking not on His own initiative and authority, but only the words He heard from Jesus (*Joh. 16:13*). We can trust Him to guide and direct us as well.

   C. Empowerment
One of the first Bible verses I ever learned was *Eph. 5:18*, talking about the Holy Spirit who would fill and empower us for daily living and service.

When Stephen preached, those in his audience *"were not able to resist the wisdom and the Spirit by which he spoke."* (*Act. 6:10*)

Paul recognized that his speech and preaching *"was not with persuasive words of human wisdom, but in demonstration of the Spirit and of power."* (*1 Cor. 2:4*) We must rely on Him, praying for Him to empower us and our message to cut through to people's hearts.

2. The Role of the Holy Spirit in Relationship to the Audience

What does the Spirit of God do in the lives of our listeners as we preach?

   A. Conviction
He convicts them of their need for Jesus, convicting them of their sin, their lack of God's righteousness and the coming judgment (*Joh. 16:8-11*).

Paul wrote in *1 The. 1:5*, *"For our gospel did not come to you in word only, but also in power, and in the Holy Spirit, and in much assurance."* The Spirit of God was at work as Paul and his companions preached the Gospel. We can trust that men and women will come to faith in Christ as the Spirit of God works in their lives.

   B. Transformation
The Spirit of God loves to transform people's lives. *"Now the Lord is the Spirit, and where the Spirit of the Lord is, there is liberty. But we all, with unveiled face, beholding as in a mirror the glory of the Lord, are being transformed into the same image from glory to glory, just as by the Spirit of the Lord."* (*2 Cor. 3:17-18*)

Paul knew that Christian growth was dependent on, initiated by, and empowered with the Spirit. *"Are you so foolish? Having begun in the Spirit, are you now being made perfect by the flesh?"* (*Gal. 3:3*).

And what is the product of the Spirit in our lives? *Gal. 5:22-23* tells us, *"But the fruit of the Spirit is love, joy, peace, longsuffering, kindness, goodness, faithfulness, gentleness, self-control."*

NOTES

3. The Role of the Holy Spirit in Relationship to the Purposes of God

A. <u>The Glory of God</u>
The Spirit of God came not to glorify Himself but to glorify the Lord Jesus. The Lord Jesus came to glorify the Father. And we are called in *1 Cor. 10:31* to glorify God in all that we do.

Paul concludes the first half of his letter to the Ephesians with these words of praise, recognizing that the purpose of the church is to bring glory to God: *"Now to Him who is able to do exceedingly abundantly above all that we ask or think, according to the power that works in us, to Him be glory in the church by Christ Jesus to all generations, forever and ever." (Eph. 3:20-21)*

B. <u>The Building Up of the Church</u>
When God designed the church, He had a unique plan and purpose for how it would grow. It would grow by the preaching of the Word. Notice what Paul says in *Eph. 4:11-16*:

And He Himself gave some to be apostles, some prophets, some evangelists, and some pastors and teachers, for the equipping of the saints for the work of ministry, for the edifying of the body of Christ, till we all come to the unity of the faith and of the knowledge of the Son of God, to a perfect man, to the measure of the stature of the fullness of Christ; that we should no longer be children, tossed to and fro and carried about with every wind of doctrine, by the trickery of men, in the cunning craftiness of deceitful plotting, but, speaking the truth in love, may grow up in all things into Him who is the head – Christ – from whom the whole body, joined and knit together by what every joint supplies, according to the effective working by which every part does its share, causes growth of the body for the edifying of itself in love.

C. <u>The Spreading of the Gospel to the Ends of the Earth</u>
Finally, the Spirit of God is committed to the spreading of the Gospel to the whole world. *Act. 1:4-8* says,

And being assembled together with them, He commanded them not to depart from Jerusalem, but to wait for the Promise of the Father, 'which,' He said, 'you have heard from Me; for John truly baptized with water, but you shall be baptized with the Holy Spirit not many days from now.' Therefore, when they had come together, they asked Him, saying, 'Lord, will You at this time restore the kingdom to Israel?' And He said to them, 'It is not for you to know times or seasons which the Father has put in His own authority. But you shall receive power when the Holy Spirit has come upon you; and you shall be witnesses of Me in Jerusalem, and in all Judea and Samaria, and to the end of the earth.'

Assignment:

Start your time with prayer that the Holy Spirit would work *in* your life and *through* your life to build His church.

Finally, what did you learn about the ministry of the Holy Spirit in this chapter?

NOTES

Chapter 14
Delivery Skills

1. What Difference Does Good Delivery Make?

A. What purpose does good delivery serve? It allows your content to be heard clearly and without any barriers. You should not be concerned about whether or not you are known as a great public speaker. You should be concerned that people understand and respond to your message.

B. Studies have been done that have asked people to describe good and bad speakers. Poor speakers were identified by their *poor quality of delivery* and *lack of a good speaking voice*. Good speakers, however, were identified by their *content*.

C. In the case of poor speakers, there was something that got in the way that prevented their content from being heard or remembered. So effective speaking delivery in your new church is simply a matter of removing stumbling blocks that get in the way of your content.

D. If you speak in public so that people hearing you become impressed with your speaking, you will not be an effective preacher. You don't call attention to yourself, but to the Word of God.

E. You should desire to speak with an intensified naturalness in your style. A good window does not call attention to itself. It merely lets in the light. A good speaker is like that. He is so natural that his hearers never notice his manner of speaking. They are conscious only of his content.

F. A good speech looks like an enlarged conversation. Think of speaking to one or two of your friends. You are telling them a story when several others join the conversation. You speak a little louder with a little more animation. Now dozens join you, and soon you have a crowd.

G. When did your story turn from a personal conversation to a speech? Obviously it was gradual. But the point is this: the most effective speaking style is a conversational style that invites people to listen to you.

2. Three Goals of Delivery

As we talk about specific delivery skills, remember these three goals:

A. Purposeful: Any delivery style can work if you know why you are doing it.

B. Natural: Your delivery style must look natural to you.

C. Varied: Nothing works if it is overdone. Using the same gesture, or the same vocal cadence, eventually becomes dull.

Let's talk briefly about four dimensions of delivery: gestures, eye contact and facial expression, voice, and posture/movement.

3. Gestures

There are three kinds of gestures:

A. Descriptive gestures demonstrate something's size, weight, direction or action.

B. Cultural gestures are unique to each culture and communicate a non-verbal message.

C. Emphatic gestures add emphasis to our speaking and reinforce the message you are communicating.

The problem of teaching delivery skills to you as a church planter is not one of superimposing additional characteristics to the communicator. Rather, it is largely one of removing unnatural movements and freeing people up to speak with the same naturalness that they display in normal, everyday conversations.

4. Eye Contact and Facial Expression

Perhaps the most important delivery skill is eye contact. Look at people as you speak to them. Know your message so well that you can concentrate on the people to whom you are speaking.

Regarding facial expressions, animate your face. Expressions are powerful! Learn to smile when you are speaking. A smile makes your voice sound pleasant.

5. Voice Quality

People sometimes have trouble pronouncing and enunciating their words. This often comes from poor speech habits learned from childhood. Here are some helpful suggestions:

A. Speak loudly enough to be heard by everyone in your audience.

B. Speak clearly. Don't have a lazy style to your speaking.

C. Vary your rate (from fast to slow), your pitch (from high to low), and your volume (from loud to soft). Use pauses in your vocal delivery.

6. Posture and Movement

A. Stand up straight and erect when speaking. Stand boldly and assuredly. Your posture communicates a message of confidence to your audience.

B. Too much movement as a communicator can be distracting. Learn to stand still and only move when there is a purpose to do so.

7. Speaking with Notes

One question church planters always ask is how many notes they should use when preaching and teaching. There are three styles. You will have to find the one that works best for you:

    A. <u>Preaching from a Manuscript</u>
A manuscript contains your speech written out word for word. The benefit of this style is that you have thought through everything you want to say and exactly how to say it. It is right there in front of you. You won't forget your speech, because it is written out right there. All you have to do is read it. But that's the problem: reading a manuscript is a terrible way of communicating with an audience. It breaks eye-contact, stifles spontaneity and generally results in a boring presentation.

Some preachers in their church plant like to write out their message word for word in preparation but then only take a few notes with them into the pulpit. This works well with many.

    B. <u>Preaching from few Notes</u>
This style uses minimal notes (enough to help you remember what you want to say), but not enough to distract you in your delivery. Those who use this approach simply carry one or two sheets of paper with them into the pulpit that contains a brief outline and perhaps a few other words that will remind them of what they want to say.

This is the method I prefer, and often times I will simply write my outline into the margins of my Bible. I find this approach frees me to be spontaneous in my delivery and to focus on those in my audience.

    C. <u>Preaching from Memory</u>
People who use this approach take no notes with them when they speak. They have simply memorized everything. I find two problems with this approach. First, it takes a lot of time to memorize an entire sermon. You have better things to do with your time. Preaching is not a contest to see who can speak with the fewest notes! The second problem is that if you forget a word, a phrase or a whole point, you can become so flustered that it can ruin your whole sermon.

Assignment:

You have just learned some of the basics of delivery skills in preaching. Pair up with one of the other students in your class and you preach a sermon. Have your fellow student evaluate your delivery skills in the following areas:

Gestures

Eye Contact and Facial Expression

Voice Quality

Posture and Movement

Speaking with Notes

Now switch places and you listen to your fellow student and evaluate his delivery skills in those same areas.

What did you learn about your delivery skills?

What are you doing well?

What area(s) do you need to work on?

Chapter 15
Growing as a Communicator

1. Developing Your Own Style

A. You are unique. There is no one in the entire world like you. From your fingerprints, the way you look, and your physical DNA, there is no one exactly like you. *Psa. 139:13-16* says that God formed our inward parts and knitted us together when we were still in our mother's womb.

God also has equipped you with spiritual gifts, a unique personality, passions, abilities, talents and experiences that make you different from anyone else in the world.

God created you to be you, not to be someone else. He has called you to serve Him through those gifts, personality, passions, abilities, talents and experiences.

God created you to be you, not someone else.

B. One of the greatest temptations in ministry is to find someone we admire and mimic them. We reason that they are successful because of the way they do what they do, and if we want to serve God successfully, we should do it just that way. This often evidences itself in our style of preaching. We copy someone who is successful, instead of being ourselves and doing it the way God has designed us.

C. Take steps to grow and mature in your preaching abilities. Here are some suggestions:
- Try new things. Don't be afraid to fail. Find out what works for you and what doesn't work for you.
- Ask for feedback and critique. Ask people to be honest with you and help you grow in your abilities. Learn from what they say. And don't forget to thank them for their contribution to your development! We understand that this can be varied within one culture, let alone various cultures. It is your high calling to contextualize so that authenticity is evident in your communication.
- Set goals. Learn new skills.
- Watch others who are successful in ministry. Encourage them – and seek to find out what makes them successful. You can learn much from people who are seasoned and effective.

A great preacher from Europe talked about how he has grown as a Biblical communicator:

> *In my early days I used to think that my business was to expound and exegete the text; I am afraid I left the application to the Holy Spirit. It is amazing how you can conceal your laziness with a little pious phraseology! The Holy Spirit certainly can and does apply the Word for the people. But it is wrong to deny our own responsibility in the application of the Word. All great preachers understand this. This is what the Puritans called 'preaching through to the heart.' This is how my own preaching has changed. I have learned to add application to exposition – and this is the bridge building across the chasm.*[25]

> **Assignment:**
>
> Read *Psa. 139:13-16* and *Rom. 12:3-8*. How has God designed you? What are your strengths? What are the areas you need to grow and develop in as a preacher?

2. Passion in Preaching

I love Arjuna Chiguluri, my friend from India. He preaches with passion. Whenever I hear him, I come away more inspired to love Jesus and more committed to serve Jesus than before.

Charles Haddon Spurgeon was known as the "prince of preachers." This great orator in 19th Century England held audiences captive as he faithfully taught the Word of God. Someone once said to him, *"I wish I could preach like you do."* Spurgeon responded, *"Young man, go out in the courtyard, pour kerosene all over your body, light a match, and people will come to watch you burn!"*[26]

That's a great story because it illustrates a great principle: we must have a passion for preaching if we are going to be effective.

I love preaching God's Word. I have a passion for it. That passion began early in my Christian life, as I realized how precious the Bible was and how much it was relevant to my life.

   A. <u>Study passionately</u>
   Just like Ezra (*7:10*) who made a decision to set his heart to study the Law of the Lord, we must do the same. I find an inner joy that wells up inside my heart when I sit down to study. I love to sit there to read, pray and seek the meaning of the passage. And I thoroughly enjoy crafting those thoughts into a sermon.

   Don't study simply to prepare a sermon, rather study to learn the meaning of the passage. Study to have your heart filled. Study because the Word of God is life itself.

> **NOTES**

Solomon, the writer of Ecclesiastes, talked about the process of study and preparation that he went through. Read this passage and notice the passion involved in the process:

In addition to being a wise man, the preacher also taught the people knowledge, and he pondered, searched out and arranged many proverbs. The preacher sought to find delightful words and to write words of truth correctly. The words of wise men are like goads, and masters of these collections are like well-driven nails. They are given by one shepherd (Ecc. 12:9-11).

Notice all the preparation involved:
- He ponders: In other words, he carefully thinks about what he will say.
- He searches out: He researches and he studies before he speaks.
- He arranges: As he searches out truths, he categorizes them. He sets things in a logical order.
- He looks for just the right words: He doesn't cut any corners by just arbitrarily picking his words.

This preacher is worth listening to because he does his study passionately!

As a result, Solomon says his words are like goads. A goad is a sharp stick that you use to guide animals. Think of it as a cattle prod. In the same way, your messages need to motivate people to do something. The Bible also says his words are like well-driven nails. The best-crafted messages make a truth memorable. Like a nail, the truth is driven in and you can't pull it out. People remember what is said. It is well driven into the minds of others, smoothly holding their thoughts into Biblical formation.

B. Preach passionately

I remember one of my professors in seminary who also served as a local pastor. Each week as it would come time for the sermon, he would stand up and literally run to the pulpit. He didn't even realize he was doing it until someone in his church pointed it out. But he said, *"I guess I am just so excited to preach the Word that I can't wait to get started!"* That's a man with a passion to communicate!

Preach with intensity. Preach with emotion. Preach with great confidence.

I get so excited when I see people's lives changed by the Word of God. Do you? The more confident you become as a student of God's Word and a communicator of His message, the more you will find a great joy in preaching.

3. Overcoming Stage Fright

People all over the world are afraid of speaking in public. Some people get extremely nervous, to the point where their body shakes and they sweat profusely. Stage fright is a universal problem. It can be controlled (but not necessarily eliminated). If you suffer from stage fright, these principles will help you:

A. Prepare well
   The most effective solution to stage fright is total preparation. Know your material so well that it produces confidence that will carry you through your nervousness.

B. Exercise physically
   Prior to getting up to speak, do some push-ups or other form of exercise to eliminate the excessive energy in your body. However, if it is really hot in your area, you may want to bring another shirt so that you are not too wet before you preach.

C. Remember the value of nervousness
   Nervous energy is a useful thing if we direct it properly. Psychologists tell us we can only feel one powerful emotion at a time. Replace your fear with determination and commitment. Turn your energy to enthusiasm rather than fear.

D. Protect your memory
   Make sure you have speaking notes that will help you remember your message.

E. Build good speaking habits
   The more we are under stress as a church planter, the more we resort to habits we have developed in the past. Therefore, build good habits in your speaking. Practice, practice and practice some more!

F. Make a commitment to the significance of your message
   We have the greatest news ever announced. To be driven to speak because of the importance of your ideas is the best way to develop confidence.

One who suffers stage fright is, literally, self-conscious, self-aware. The speaker who speaks because he is committed to God's truth, not his own self-importance, will want to speak, and can do it whole-heartedly.

The plan for confidence in speaking is:
Confidence = Competence + Commitment!

Chapter 16
Five Warnings to Preachers

1. Warning # 1 – The Danger of Speaking for God

The Apostle James tells his readers, *"Let not many of you become teachers, knowing that we shall receive a stricter judgment."* (*3:1*). As leaders and teachers of the Word of God, we are held to a higher standard and are subject to a stricter judgment. That means we must approach the Bible with seriousness and humility.

As a preacher, you are held responsible for what you preach and teach. Watch your doctrine closely. Do not play with the Bible. Every day, remind yourself you are nothing more than a servant, saved by grace, who has the privilege of serving his Lord.

Two servants of God in the New Testament thought they were indispensible. They arrogantly thought it was "all about them."

And in *1 Tim. 1:20*, Paul wrote out his indictment against them: *"Among these are Hymenaeus and Alexander, whom I have handed over to Satan, so that they will be taught not to blaspheme."*

Forever their names are recorded in Biblical history as men who became disqualified for ministry because of their sinful attitudes.

2. Warning # 2 – Pride

Standing up in front of people preaching the Word of God can be intoxicating. Like a drug that gives us an emotional and/or physical high, preaching can literally "go to our heads." One of the greatest dangers for those of us who do a lot of preaching is that we must remain humble.

    A. <u>The danger of pride</u>
    "For all that is in the world – the lust of the flesh, the lust of the eyes, and the pride of life – is not of the Father but is of the world." (*1 Joh. 2:16*)
    "Boast no more so very proudly, do not let arrogance come out of your mouth; for the Lord is a God of knowledge, and with Him actions are weighed." (*1 Sam. 2:3*)

    B. <u>The solution to pride</u>
    "But He gives more grace. Therefore He says: God resists the proud but gives grace to the humble…Humble yourselves in the sight of the Lord, and He will lift you up." (*Jam. 4:6, 10*)

3. Warning # 3 – Self-Sufficiency

There is an interesting paradox. The more God uses us, the more grace He extends to us. However, it is easy for us to come to the conclusion that *we are* the ones responsible for our success. Nothing could be further from the truth!

In the book of 2 Corinthians, Paul lays out his philosophy of ministry. And early on he states that the power of ministry comes *not from us* but from *God*. Paul writes,

> "And we have such trust through Christ toward God. Not that we are sufficient of ourselves to think of anything as being from ourselves, but our sufficiency is from God, who also made us sufficient as ministers of the new covenant, not of the letter but of the Spirit; for the letter kills, but the Spirit gives life." (2 Cor. 3:4-6)

We must remember Jesus' words: *"Apart from Me you can do nothing."* (Joh. 15:5)

4. Warning # 4 – Losing Your First Love

I have already brought up the danger of losing your first love (see chapter 5). This is the greatest danger for those of in professional ministry. It is so easy to "look good" on the outside, but to have cold and tired hearts on the inside.

To be sure, there are times when we are emotionally "down." It is during these times that we must persevere in our study of the Word. Our people demand our best efforts. I have often found that it is when I am most emotionally empty that I must work the hardest. But the gift is that when I do that, God meets me and encourages my heart.

Here are three suggestions to keep your relationship with Jesus at the center of your life.

A. Don't tolerate sin in your life. Don't give it a "place."
Eph. 4:27 tells us not to give the devil an opportunity in our lives. The word opportunity literally means a "place," or a "foothold." It is from there that Satan can exert great influence.

Keep short accounts with God by continually confessing your sins (*1 Joh. 1:9*).

Heb. 12:15 cautions us not to allow a root of bitterness to well up in our lives.

B. Guard your devotional times
Make sure you are not studying the Word simply "to get a sermon." Study for your heart and soul's enrichment. *Love God with all your heart, soul, mind and strength.*

C. Be accountable to other men to make sure you are serving Jesus out of good motives. Be honest with them. Accountability is useless unless you open your heart and receive their counsel and correction.

5. Warning # 5 – Loving the Praise of Men

You preach "for an audience of One." God is the only One we can look to for affirmation and the statement, *"Well done, good and faithful servant."* Unfortunately, we get it reversed and start looking to men for their praise and affirmation. In *Joh. 12:43*, Jesus scolded the Pharisees for *"loving the praise from men more than praise from God."*

NOTES

Assignment:

This chapter contains some very serious advice for church planters and Christian leaders. Take each of the 5 points in this chapter and pray for thirty minutes, spending 5-6 minutes over each point.

As you pray, evaluate your own soul, asking the Spirit of God to convict you of sin where necessary, to strengthen your resolve and commitment where needed, and to give you to boldness to model and proclaim the Gospel in your new church plant.

Chapter 17
Developing and Training Others to Preach

1. Introduction

Act. 13:1-3 is one of my favorite passages from the New Testament. It is directly relevant to church planters, because it begins with the Holy Spirit directing the leaders of the church at Antioch to consecrate their best men for a missionary enterprise of church planting.

> *Now in the church that was at Antioch there were certain prophets and teachers: Barnabas, Simeon who was called Niger, Lucius of Cyrene, Manaen who had been brought up with Herod the Tetrarch, and Saul (who was later known as Paul). As they ministered to the Lord and fasted, the Holy Spirit said, 'Now separate to Me Barnabas and Saul for the work to which I have called them.' Then, having fasted and prayed and laid hands on them, they sent them away.*

What a teaching team they had in that church! These six men were astounding Bible teachers. In fact, Saul (Paul) is listed last, as if to say he was the most inexperienced!

God the Holy Spirit comes along and says, in effect, *"What you are doing at Antioch is good, but I want to expand it all across Asia Minor."* I think that was a hard word to hear. Yes, it was exciting to think of what God was going to do. But it was hard for them to lose two of the men who were their leaders.

But please note: they released them, prayed for them, laid hands on them, and sent them on their way.

The Church at Antioch had a great teaching team. It wasn't simply one man. There was a shared preaching ministry. And I think there is something very Biblical to that which we want to reflect on today.

Very likely you are the only man trained to preach in your situation. That is okay for now, as it was for Barnabas. But part of your job is to find, develop and train others to preach also.

2. Reproducing Yourself

2 Tim. 2:2 is a verse that TTI has built its ministry on. The Timothy Initiative is named after this verse. It says, *"And the things that you have heard from me among many witnesses, commit these to faithful men who will be able to teach others also."*

In that one verse are listed four generations of leaders:

> Paul, Timothy, Faithful men, Others also.

NOTES

Think about that. Paul had built his life into Timothy (and dozens of others like Silas, Sosthenes, and Epaphroditus). Timothy was called to reproduce his life into "faithful men," men who would grow as leaders and ultimately reproduce their lives into "others also."

So my question to you is: *who are you training?* Who are the "church-planters-to-be" you are raising up? If they don't come from your ministry, where are they going to come from?

3. Team Preaching

A. One of the things you will need to do is to train these men to preach, just like you are being trained to preach. Give these young men a chance. Many of them will do very well. A few of them may even surpass you in their ministry abilities. That's great! Be secure in your own calling and abilities, like Barnabas was, as he freed up Paul to eventually pass him.

B. Benefits of Team Preaching
- You develop new leaders and give them a chance to grow.
- They will use their gifts to help build up your church.
- It gives you an opportunity to rest from preaching and re-energize your spiritual life.
- Your congregation doesn't hear from just one voice. They hear from a team of several men, each of whom has unique gifts and abilities. This expands the spiritual diet.
- Those men will grow in experience and after a season of training, they will be ready to launch out as church planters with a team.

Chapter 18
Questions and Answers

Question: "I'm just beginning as a preacher. How can I improve?"

First, work hard. Every great church planting preacher I have known has had to work hard, both in the study and in their development as a preacher.

Second, preach often. Experience is a great teacher.

Third, get feedback. Be open to others' critique. Don't be defensive. Learn from your mistakes.

Question: "How long does it take you to prepare a sermon?"

I spend less time now than I did earlier in my ministry. I used to spend about fifteen hours on a sermon, but now it is closer to eight to ten hours. Over the years of my ministry, I've accumulated more information, more knowledge of the Scriptures, and more Bible study skills, and many more stories and illustrations.

Question: "What's your critique of expository preaching today?"

I just read an interview in *Preaching Magazine* with a pastor known around the world. I'll let his words answer this question. He said,

The question of 'so what?' is so important today. I don't think expository preaching suffers because it's the wrong method. I think it suffers because it's not done very well by some people who attempt it. They make it dry and boring. If that happens, it's unforgivable – how can you make the living Word of God dry and boring? Until we've dealt with the "so what" and "now what" questions, we haven't completed our preaching assignment. People don't need a better set of notes – they need to know how the Word of God is going to work in their lives.

Question: "Do you practice your sermons before you deliver them?"

I know many preachers that do practice their sermons during the week. But my answer is no, I don't. I find practicing a sermon quite artificial. I'm talking to myself, not to people. And that tends to take away the power and sense of urgency.

But I do one thing that is helpful: As I'm working on my sermon all week long, I'll look for opportunities to tell people what I am learning. During the week I will have many personal meetings where I'll share some of the insights from my study. Perhaps it will be a certain principle from a verse. Other times it might be an illustration or an application point that may make its way into my sermon. The two parts of my sermon I will give quite a bit of attention to are my opening remarks (the first one or two sentences), and my conclusion. I find if I get started well and end well; the middle usually goes pretty well.

NOTES

Question: "How long should a sermon be?"

As long as it takes to cover the passage adequately! I know some preachers who speak for over an hour. You better be very good if you're going to speak that long! On the other hand, I know some who do an excellent job in 30 or 35 minutes. Personally, I usually speak for 40-45 minutes. That's just my style, and, of course, a reflection of my culture.

You will have to determine what works for you and what is best for those in your culture. But remember this: if you are enflamed with the Word of God, and deliver it in a compelling manner, people will listen to you for a long time.

Question: "I've been told that if I am nervous when I am speaking, I should not look at my audience. I should look over their heads to the back of the room. What do you think?"

I think that's crazy. It's as crazy as saying that if you get nervous while driving a car, bike or motorcycle, you should close your eyes! The results are disastrous.

There are better ways of dealing with nervousness than refusing to look at our audience. We are called to preach to people. How many times in Jesus' ministry did people notice His look of compassion for them? (See *Mat. 9:36*) Develop the habit of good eye-contact, both in personal conversations and in public speaking.

Assignment:

List other questions that you would like to address to your training center leader for his answers.

Appendix 1
Sermon Outlines

As we have discussed previously in this book, there are many ways to preach Biblical sermons. I have collected examples from church planting leaders around the world to give you insight into their style.

SERMON #1

This first sermon is an example of a topical sermon. The author, a church planter with experience in Africa and Asia, wanted to focus on the impact of Jesus' death on the cross, helping his audience to understand more fully what Jesus accomplished by dying for us. He uses a variety of New Testament Scriptures to build a *theology* of Christ's sacrifice.

Title: God Isn't Mad Any More! (What Jesus' Death Accomplished for You and Me), Various Scriptures.

Introduction

Jesus was like a breath of fresh air among the religious leaders of His day (and of all time). He was winsome, attractive, and positive. He was unlike anyone else. He was unique and extraordinary in His life. But He was even more unique and extraordinary in His death.

Luke 9:51: "As the time approached for him to be taken up to heaven, Jesus resolutely set out for Jerusalem."

In dying, Jesus died the death of deaths – like none other.

1. His Death Was A True Sacrifice

His death was the innocent for the guilty, the pure for the impure.

Mark 10:45: "For even the Son of Man did not come to be served, but to serve, and to give His life as a ransom for many."

This verse tells us Jesus' job description.

Jesus' death was agony:

Hebrews 12:2: "Let us fix our eyes on Jesus, the author and perfecter of our faith, who for the joy set before Him endured the cross, scorning its shame, and sat down at the right hand of the throne of God."

Matthew 27:46: "About the ninth hour Jesus cried out in a loud voice, 'Eloi, Eloi, lama sabachthani?' — which means, 'My God, my God, why have you forsaken me?'"

For the first time in eternity, the Son was separated from the Father. For the first time in eternity, the Father was separated from the Son. Why? For you, and for me! God's justice was satisfied by Jesus' death on the cross.

2. His Death Accomplished Our Salvation

1 John 2:1-2: "My dear children, I write this to you so that you will not sin. But if anybody does sin, we have one who speaks to the Father in our defense - Jesus Christ, the Righteous One. He is the atoning sacrifice for our sins, and not only for ours but also for the sins of the whole world."

This verse tells me three things:
- His death not only made salvation possible – it accomplished salvation for us.
- We have a defense attorney in heaven – we can stand against the accusations of Satan.
- His death atoned for our sins – once and for all

If God did it, then it makes my salvation secure!

3. His Death Was a Full Payment

John 19:30: "When he had received the drink, Jesus said, 'It is finished.' With that, he bowed his head and gave up His spirit."

Colossians 2:13-14: "When you were dead in your sins and in the uncircumcision of your sinful nature, God made you alive with Christ. He forgave us all our sins, having canceled the written code, with its regulations, that was against us and that stood opposed to us; He took it away, nailing it to the cross."

Conclusion

What does Jesus' death mean for me? What does it mean for you? Because I have believed in Christ and trusted Him as the payment for my sins, there are three specific truths that can be applied to my life:
- I am part of God's forever family.
- I am completely forgiven.
- I have a new heart and a clean start.

Jesus' death on the cross means God isn't mad at me anymore! Our God is the God of the second chance – and the third chance – and the fourth chance!

SERMON #2

This sermon, by a church planting leader in South America, is an example of taking a narrative passage (*Acts 27*) and bringing life-related principles to bear to his audience.

Title: "Weathering a Shipwreck"
Passage: *Acts 27*

Introduction

Our lives can be shipwrecked by a series of bad choices. What will enable us to live successfully and remain true to the Lord Jesus Christ?

1. Allow the Lord to warn you – *Acts 27:9-13*

- Misleading pressures – *Acts 27:5-9*.
- Misguided counselors – *Acts 27:10-11*.
- Mistaken priorities – *Acts 27:12; 1 Timothy 1:18-19*.
- Misdirected majority – *Acts 27:12*.
- Misread circumstances – *Acts 27:13*.

2. Trust the Lord to protect you – *Acts 27:14-24*

- *Luke 21:16-18*.
- *2 Timothy 4:18*.
- *Romans 8:35-39*.

3. Ask the Lord to encourage you – *Acts 27:23-25*

- *Romans 15:4*.
- *Isaiah 41:10*.
- *Hebrews 13:5-6*.

4. Expect the Lord to guide you – *Acts 27:24-26*

- *Acts 23:11*.
- *Acts 28:14*.
- *Ephesians 2:10*.
- *Romans 8:28-30*.

SERMON #3

Some sermons are meant to encourage. Some are meant to challenge and motivate. Still others are meant to convict their listeners of sin. This sermon not only convicts the listeners – it convicts the preacher to make sure he is not neglecting or drifting from an intimate relationship with Jesus.

Sermon Title: "Don't Neglect... Don't Even Drift"
Passage: *Hebrews 2:1-4*

Introduction

This passage in the book of Hebrews talks about two dangers Christians face: drifting and neglecting.

Danger #1 – Drifting

Drift away – this word can be used of something flowing or slipping past, as of a ring slipping off a finger. It can be used of something slipping down and getting caught in a difficult place. It is used of something which carelessly has been allowed to slip away. It is often used of a ship that has been allowed to drift past the harbor because a sailor forgot to attend to the steerage or to properly chart the wind, tides, and current.

That can happen to Christians who do not passionately pursue Jesus every day of their lives.

What are signs that an individual Christian is drifting?
What are signs that a church is drifting?
What do you struggle with? How are you tempted to drift?

Danger #2 – Neglecting

What does it mean to neglect something? I looked up the word neglect in a dictionary and it gave two primary meanings:
- To give little attention or respect to; to disregard.
- To leave undone or unattended to especially through carelessness.

Synonyms of the word neglect are: to disregard, ignore, overlook, slight, and forget. It means to pass over without giving due attention.

In V*ine's Expository Dictionary of New Testament Words* this word is defined as *being careless or not to care, to make light of something*.

Hebrews 2 tells us that we have a sure and certain revelation from God about His will for our lives, ministry and our walk with Jesus. The issue is not whether we have God's revelation or not, but are we drifting away and neglecting Him in the way we live?

There are four key points in insuring that we do not neglect God's revelation:

1. **Absorbing what we have heard is more essential than seeking something new.**
   - There is a trap that Christians fall into where they seek something more than Jesus. "The basics" of the Christian faith are not something you learn and then move away from. They are the basics in the sense that they are foundational for everything else that is built upon them.
   - You never grow too old to be reminded of the basics and to return to them in obedience. Peter writes in *2 Peter 1:12* that he would always be ready to remind his listeners of the basics. His reasoning was that even though they already knew the basics, and that they were established in the basic truths that were present in their lives, there was always benefit to being reminded of them.
   - Absorbing what we have heard is more essential than seeking something new.

2. **Overcoming the peril of drifting requires the discipline of application.**
   - When we're under pressure, drifting starts when we rely on our own instincts rather than on the seasoned truth of Scripture.
   - When making decisions, the currents become deadly because we value human ingenuity and opinion more than God's truth.
   - When battling some turbulent sea in our lives, we are in danger of ending up on the reefs because we opt for what is comfortable, though wrong, instead of what is painful, though right.

3. **Obeying God's deliverance plan is still the only means of lasting satisfaction in life.**
   - "Trust and Obey" is the title to a famous old hymn of the faith. Its refrain says, *Trust and obey, for there's no other way, to be happy in Jesus, than to trust and obey.*
   - When we trust God with every detail of our lives, He will infuse our lives with joy and satisfaction.

4. **Neglecting God's deliverance plan inevitably leads to inescapable consequences.**
   - We cannot disobey God without suffering dangerous consequences.
   - Where will you be spiritually in ten years? In twenty years? Will you be walking with Jesus? Will you still continue to obey Him and trust Him as Lord of your life? Or will you neglect and drift and fall away?

Conclusion

William Barclay in his commentary, The Letter to the Hebrews, writes:
For most of us the threat of life is not so much that we should plunge into disaster, but that we should drift into sin. There are few people who deliberately and in a moment turn their backs on God; there are many who day by day drift farther and farther away from Him. There are not many who in one moment of time commit some disastrous sin; there are many who almost imperceptibly involve themselves in some situation and suddenly awake to find that they have ruined life for themselves and broken someone else's heart. We must be continually on the alert against the peril of the drifting life.

NOTES

SERMON #4

Ask Christians to turn to *The Great Commission*, and most of them will locate Matthew 28:18-20. However, that is only one of at least five times Jesus gave His disciples the command to go into all the world. This sermon, originally given in India, to 200 church planters at the International Church Planters Summit, shows the uniqueness of each of these commands.

Title: "Jesus' Commands for Us" - A Fresh Look at the Great Commission in Five Passages.
Passages: *John 20:21; Mark 16:15; Matthew 28:18-20; Luke 24:44-49; Acts 1:8.*

Introduction

A mission is a task we have been given to accomplish. A co-mission is a task we have been given to accomplish in partnership with someone else as a partner.

Jesus is our partner in the *Great Commission*.

Eph 3:10 tells us that God's plan is that His manifold wisdom might be made known through the church. How will the world know of His manifold wisdom? By us following the Great Commission and going into all the world.

1. We Are Sent – *John 20:21*
- We serve the God who sends His people to all cultures in the world.
- With God, there are no locked doors. He opens the doors so the Gospel may be proclaimed everywhere.
- There are many different cultures in the world. We are sent to all of them. Therefore, we must not only know God, but also understand the culture(s) to which He is sending us.
- Church planting is key
- The Great Commission is always accompanied by the presence of the Holy Spirit or the promise of His presence with us.

2. To Everyone Everywhere – *Mark 16:15*
- We are sent to reach every man, woman and child in the world.
- However, we all have circles of influence in our lives made up of people we know, people we live nearby, our family and friends, and people we work with.
- Churches also have circles of influence, and they are accountable to reach the people in those circles.
- In Paul's ministry, he said *imitate me*! What did Paul do?
- In the book of Acts, he demonstrated many unique approaches to reach unique people groups. In Paul's ministry, there were different beginning points. But he always ended up at the same ending point; preaching the death and resurrection of Christ.

3. **With A Strategy** – *Matthew 28:18-20*
    - Jesus said He has all authority in heaven and earth.
    - He commanded us to make disciples – that is the primary verb in the Great Commission in *Matthew 28*. There are three words that qualify how we are to make disciples.
        - ▶ *Going* – this speaks of evangelism and telling others how they can know Jesus personally.
        - ▶ *Baptizing* – baptism is how people become a part of a local church. They are now relationally connected to others who can help them grow as a follower of Jesus.
        - ▶ *Teaching* – this is the educational aspect of the Commission. We are to teach new believers all that Jesus commanded us. As a result, they will become personally equipped and will begin to mature as a disciple.

4. **Telling a Message** – *Luke 24:44-49*
    - The message we are to proclaim is the Gospel of repentance from sin and faith in Jesus.
    - There is no other message in heaven and on earth by which men can be saved – *Acts 4:12; 2 Corinthians 5:18-20*.

5. **Empowered for the Task** – *Acts 1:8*
    - How are believers equipped for this mission? The necessary tool is the empowering of the Holy Spirit.
    - We must be focused on the right things. Acts 1:5-7 tells us the right thing is not prophecy and when Jesus will return, but it is the mission He has given us. We must trust the work of the Holy Spirit in the lives of new believers, new pastors, and new churches.
    - We must be focused on the right places. Jesus talks about Jerusalem, Judea, Samaria and the ends of the earth. There is a logical progression and strategy involved here.

Conclusion

We are sent…to everyone everywhere…with a strategy…telling a message…empowered for the task.

Will you commit to this Great Commission? Will your new church be committed to this Great Commission?

> **NOTES**

SERMON #5

Some Bible passages can yield more than one sermon. Sermons #5 and #6 are examples of two messages taken from the same passage. Preached by a church planter in Asia, they show us what it is like to see a passage from two different perspectives.

Title: "Jesus the Servant"
Passage: *John 13:1-11*

1. **Jesus Serves Us Because He Loves Us**
    - The hour had come:
        - ▶ Since – Miracle at Cana – the time had not come
        - ▶ Now – the time has come to leave the World and return to the Father.
    - Jesus' love for his own:
        - ▶ Up to now – the focus has been on God's love for the world.
        - ▶ Now – in sight of the Cross – special focus on those who are his own.
    - Love that goes the distance:
        - ▶ He "Loved them to the end."
        - ▶ Jesus loved all the way – by going to the cross.
        - ▶ Washing their feet is a picture of the atoning work on the Cross.

2. **Jesus, Lord and Master, Becomes a Slave**
    - The power and glory of position:
        - ▶ Jesus knew who he was – and what he was - He was Master, Lord, King.
        - ▶ God had put all power and authority in his hands.
        - ▶ The glory that goes with position.
        - ▶ He has a right to glory – respect, honor, worship.
    - The shame of a slave
        - ▶ Jesus – lays aside his clothes.
        - ▶ He sets aside the mantle of glory.
        - ▶ He lays aside the out-ward displays and rights.
        - ▶ He puts on the work clothes of a slave.
        - ▶ Putting of the cloak of the Majestic and mighty Lion – taking on the garments of a stupid sheep.
    - The humble task of serving
        - ▶ Jesus does not simply serve them.
        - ▶ He serves them as a slave – at the lowest level.
        - ▶ He places himself – at the lowest point below them.

3. **The Cleansing Work of the Servant**
    - Jesus washes them - A picture of his cleansing work on the cross.
    - Peter's protest. In light of the cross – we cannot be one of his, with this work of cleansing. Only through the Cross can we be made clean
        - ▶ The daily work of the servant. There is only need for one complete washing. But – we still need daily foot washing. Jesus still serves us daily, taking up his towel and washing our dirty feet

4. Becoming Sin for Us
- Was it really necessary to go to such extremes? Did Jesus really need to go all the way to the bottom to save us? The Shame of the Cross: it was the lowest, most degrading, most dehumanizing form of death ever.
- The Shame of sin: He had to go as low as we were to elevate us as high as He is.
- He became sin and shame so that we might become the righteousness of Christ

Conclusion

Jesus, your Lord and Master, became a servant for you. What is your response?

Jesus, your Lord and Master, has modeled for you what it means to be a servant. How are you going to serve your new church?

SERMON #6

Title: "Serving Like Jesus"
Passage: *John 13:1-17*

1. **Teaching by Example**
   - Good teaching begins by modeling:
     - Jesus teaches by demonstrating truth in action.
     - Not enough to teach we must also show!
     - If you want to teach others, you must model it.
     - Do we model all that we teach and proclaim in ministry?
   - The model of servant leadership:
     - Jesus was not simply how to be a good.
     - What he is really modeling is not Serving – but leading!
   - The standard Jesus sets:
     - His service is the standard of what is expected for all his followers.
     - Jesus sets the standard – if we do not follow that standard – we are really not his follower.

2. **The Motive of Service**
   - Serving like Jesus requires loving like Jesus:
     - Christ-like serving begins with loving people.
     - Jesus loved his own, and took love to the very end, by serving.
     - It is easy to serve with wrong motives.
     - Martha – serving with a bad attitude.
     - Other wrong motives - self-righteousness, as martyrs, to manipulate others, because we feel guilty.
     - All our service – must be from a deep desire to Love God, by loving people and giving ourselves to them!
   - Serving begins at home:
     - We live in "Circles of relationship" (family, closest friends, community of faith, co-workers, neighbors, etc).
     - Jesus focused more of his love and service on the inner-circles.
       - The difficulty of serving those close to us:
     - It is often the most difficult to serve those close to us.
     - He serves us - who are no better than Judas, apart from grace.
     - It's not easy serving people who annoy us, hate us, or are mean to us.

3. **The Responsibility of Service**
   - Serving in our realm of leadership:
     - Everyone has been given leadership over something!
     - Serving is not giving up that role of leadership!
   - Laying aside the glory of your position:
     - Laying aside the glory and status of position.
     - The world loves all the prestige and fringe benefits of position.
     - We must lay aside all of that.
   - Serving those we are leading
     - We are all supposed to serve those over us.
     - It is radically different to serve those under us.
     - That is the heart of Jesus example.

SERMON # 7

The story of David killing Goliath is one of the most exciting stories in the Old Testament. We can learn much from this story as it relates to our personal lives, because each of us faces giants in our own lives. We can also learn much as we are beginning a new church. God is challenging us to live by faith. What are the "faith-lessons" that we can learn from this story?

Title: "Giant-Killing Faith: David"
Passage: *Hebrews 11:32-34; I Samuel 17*

1. **Giant-Killers serve humbly**
   1 Samuel 16:19; 17:15-24

2. **Giant-Killers maintain perspective**
   1 Samuel 17:25-27; Hebrews 12:2

3. **Giant-Killers overcome opposition**
   1 Samuel 17:28-44

4. **Giant-Killers glorify God**
   1 Samuel 17:45-47; Ephesians 3:20-21; 1 Corinthians 10:31

5. **Giant-Killers finish strong**
   1 Samuel 17:48-51

Conclusion

God calls us to live by faith. Starting a new church is one of the most challenging ministry situations. As we grow this new work, what do *you* need to do to demonstrate you are living by faith?

NOTES

SERMON #8

Jesus is our example in all of life and ministry. This sermon examines Jesus' ministry by looking at a sermon He preached in His hometown of Nazareth.

Title: "Jesus' Job Description"
Passage: *Luke 4:14-30*

1. **His Job Description – *Luke 4:17-21***
   - He Was Empowered by the Spirit of God.
   - He Proclaimed the Gospel of God.

2. **The Crowd's Reaction – *Luke 4:22-30***
   - Home-town pride – *4:22* - *"speaking well."*
   - Rebellious Opposition – *4:28* - *"furious with rage."*

3. **Following Jesus (application)**
   - Depend on God for spiritual strength.
     2 Corinthians 12:7-10
   - Proclaim the Gospel faithfully and accurately.
     Colossians 4:2-4
   - Care more about what God thinks and less about what other people think.
     Galatians 1:10
   - Live freely, focusing on God's grace.
     Romans 8:2, 14, 16
   - Allow God to fulfill His purpose in and through my life.
     John 17:4

SERMON #9

This sermon takes Paul's last words to Timothy to help the audience focus on living with an eternal perspective.

Title: "Living for the Line"
Passage: *2 Timothy 4:1-8*

Introduction

Life gets hard - and sometimes in the middle of life, we lose perspective. To follow Jesus fully, you must have an eternal perspective. *2 Corinthians 11:23-27*.

How did Paul live so successfully? He had perspective in the midst of life. Read *2 Timothy 4:6-8*.

The mark of a successful person is not how you begin the race, but how you finish.

1. We Must be Self-Disciplined - *"I have fought the good fight"*
- Fought - agony, struggle.
- The Christian life is not easy.
    - ▶ We fight against the World - pressures, temptations.
    - ▶ We fight against the Flesh - allurement of sin.
    - ▶ We fight against the Devil - spiritual battle.
- We must exhibit Self Discipline in our lives.
- Key: Perspective – *2 Corinthians 4:17-18*.

2. We Must be Goal-Oriented - *"I have finished the course"*
- Finished – wouldn't you like to be able to say that at the end?
- This doesn't happen at the end of your life. It happens early on because of the CHOICES we make.
- *Phi. 3:13-14* – Paul was focused on the finish line. He could say at the end of his life that he finished the Course.
    - ▶ Paul completed God's plan for him.
    - ▶ Do you know God's plan for you?
    - ▶ It's a matter of choices. We must choose to continue to grow in our Christian life – *Hebrews 5:13-14*
- *1 Corinthians 9:24-27*.
- Making the right choices:
    - ▶ Choosing the Right Priorities.
    - ▶ Choosing Jesus – focusing on Him.

3. We Must be Word-Centered - *"I have kept the faith"*
- To maintain perspective means being WORD CENTERED.
- The Importance of the Word of God: *2 Tim. 4:3-4*.
- Benefits: *Act. 20:24-27*
- Principle: God will always take you further than you expect. He encourages us, challenges us, and even pushes us to be the people He wants us to be. He wants us to be people who leave a legacy.

NOTES

SERMON #10

This sermon was the first in a series from the book of Acts. This church planter wanted his audience to understand ministry from the New Testament and was using the book of Acts to teach those Biblical principles. Though this sermon has many points (16 main points), it focuses clearly on one thing: we can learn how to lead and disciple the leaders in our church by following the example of Jesus. This sermon has application points built into it throughout the entire message.

Title: "How Jesus Prepared His Men for Pentecost"
Passage: *Acts 1:1-14*

1. By example
- *"All that Jesus began to do and teach…"*
- He prepared them by what He did.
- One of the key principles of ministry is that "Discipleship is caught, not taught."
- Be consistent in your own Bible study.
- Pray with the men you are discipling.
- Be an example to them.

2. By teaching
- *"To teach"* means to impart a specific body of content. Jesus had a plan on what to share with His men. He knew what He wanted to teach them.
- *v. 3* – He taught them about the kingdom. Help develop a kingdom mentality in the lives of your disciples– *Matthew 13*.
- *v. 4* – He taught the promises of God.
- *v. 5, 8* – He taught the ministry of the Holy Spirit.
- *v. 8* – He taught them His purposes and objective: to reach the world with the Gospel.

3. By working
- He worked with them until the very last day.
- *John 17:4* – *"I have finished the work You have given me to do."*
- We work until He calls us home.

4. By giving orders
- Give people direction. People need to be told what to do.
- Understand the various cultural differences – but don't back away from giving people direction.
- How? Be committed to Jesus so much that people are compelled to follow Him!

5. By living filled with the Spirit
- This is the basis of all that we do

6. By being available
- Are you available to people? If you are sold out to the Lord you will be sold out to people.

- *He presented Himself alive.*
- Have I made a total once for all irrevocable commitment to other people?
- The best way to know if you have made that commitment to God!

7. **By showing them God's life**
    - He was *Alive* – literally, *living*.
    - Let them see Jesus Christ in your life.
    - They can read about what a spirit-filled Christian is in a book. But what will attract them is to see it in you!

8. **By the resurrection and appearances**
    - It took 40 days to prove to the disciples that He was alive– *"many convincing proofs."*
    - Prove to others that Jesus is alive in you – that will attract them to Him.

9. **By building expectations**
    - He told them to wait – to be in expectation about
    - Live life expectantly, knowing God is going to do something in your life.

10. **By making them into a team**
    - The key word here is "together" – prepare people together.
    - In the Gospels, Jesus did not spend time alone with any one disciple. He spent time with the GROUP of disciples.
    - He even rebuked Peter in front of the entire group.
    - Minister to people in small groups.

11. **By letting them ask questions**

12. **By refocusing their attention**
    - Straighten out wrong thought patterns and focusing on the purpose at hand.
    - He told them, "You're thinking along the wrong lines."

13. **By imparting vision for the world**

14. **By giving them a strategy**
    - He taught them how to reach the world with the Gospel.
    - He gave them the strategy of going from Jerusalem to Judea and Samaria and ultimately to the entire world.

15. **By sending the Holy Spirit to help**

16. **By allowing them to participate in what was most important to Him**
    - Reaching the world was Jesus' ultimate goal. He enlisted them to follow and give their lives to that cause.
    - Jesus came to give His life a ransom for many, that millions could have eternal life.
    - Recruit others to follow you as you follow Jesus.
    - *Psa. 78:8-9* – They had all the equipment then needed, but in the day of battle they turned back because their hearts were not prepared and they were not faithful to God.
    - *2 Tim 2:20-22* – are we cleansed, ready for every good work? Are we available?

Appendix 2
Web-based Resources

For those of you who have access to the Internet, I have provided a list of web sites that contain preaching resources and examples.

www.centralpc.org/current_sermons
www.crmbc.org
www.danielakin.com
www.desiringgod.org
www.executableoutlines.com
www.graceglobalnetwork.org
www.intothyword.org
www.lifechurch.tv
www.marshillchurch.org/media/featured
www.mppc.org/learn/sermons
www.open.lifechurch.tv
www.pastors.com
www.preachingsermons.logos.com
www.preachingtodaysermons.com
www.preceptaustin.org
www.resurgence.com
www.saddlebackresources.com/en-US/Sermons/ SermonsHome.htm
www.sermonindex.net/
www.sermons.logos.com
www.studylight.org
www.thegospelcoalition.org/resources
www.thirdmill.org
www.ttionline.org
www.wacriswell.com

End Notes

1. Throughout this book, you will see outlines and examples of expository teaching and preaching. This one comes from a recent seminar I presented on Biblical preaching.
2. This is my personal definition of Biblical preaching. However, I am indebted to a number of people for their contribution to my thinking in this area, most notably John Shumate and Haddon Robinson.
3. John R. W. Stott, *Between Two Worlds: The Challenge of Preaching Today*, Wm. B. Eerdmans, p. 16.
4. This is a very popular quotation, and has been attributed to many people. I first heard it from Randy Marshall in a preaching course at *The Institute of Biblical Studies*.
5. Personal interview with Charles R. Swindoll, Keystone, Colorado.
6. TightRope Communications research files.
7. Tim Timmons, *How to Speak So People Will Listen*, unpublished manuscript.
8. The material in this chapter was adapted from Rick Warren's seminar on communication entitled *"Preaching for Life Change."*
9. Quoted by Haddon Robinson, *Biblical Preaching*, Baker Academic, p. 203.
10. Please see www.GraceGlobalNetwork.org and www.ttionline.org for more information about the International Church Planter Summits.
11. Darrin Patrick, blog post at www.acts29network.org/acts-29-blog, June 2, 2010.
12. Ibid.
13. Earl D. Radmacher, *Hermeneutics*, TTI Publications, p. 7.
14. John MacArthur, *Gospel of John Verse by Verse Outline Studies*, pp. 191-192.
15. Charles Swindoll, *Following Christ, The Man of God, A Study of John 6-14*, pp. 91-94.
16. Walter Kaiser, *Toward an Exegetical Theology*, Baker Books, p, 144-148.
17. Bruce Wilkinson, from a seminar sponsored by *Walk Thru The Bible*.
18. John R. W. Stott, *Guard The Gospel*, Inter Varsity Press, p. 103.
19. R. C. Sproul, from a doctoral class in *Preaching* at Reformed Theological Seminary.
20. Bruce Wilkinson, *The Seven Laws of the Learner*, Multnomah Press, (7-9).
21. Haddon Robinson, *Biblical Preaching*, Baker Academic, p. 102-103.
22. The material in this chapter was adapted from Rick Warren's article from Pastors.com entitled *"Sermon Points That Make a Point."*
23. As quoted by Henry Oursler, *How to Talk So People Will Listen*, p. 123.
24. John MacArthur, Preaching: *How to Preach Biblically*, Thomas Nelson Publishers, p, 78.
25. Michael Duduit, *Preaching the 'So What' of the Sermon*, internet blog resource. www.MichaelDuduit.com.
26. Randy Marshall, *Preaching Course*, International School of Theology.

Made in the USA
Columbia, SC
26 May 2018